W

YOUR CHURCH~ THEIR TARGET

"WHAT'S GOING ON IN THE PROTESTANT CHURCHES"

This Unbelieveable True Story Told By Eminent Authorities

A Symposium by

> *Dr. Harry R. Butman*
>
> *Reverend Irving E. Howard*
>
> *Reverend T. Robert Ingram*
>
> *Kenneth W. Ingwalson*
>
> *Dr. Howard E. Kershner*
>
> *Dr. James DeForest Murch*
>
> *Reverend Edmund A. Opitz*
>
> *Reverend Herman Otten*
>
> *Herbert A. Philbrick*
>
> *Dr. Charles S. Poling*
>
> *Reverend Rousas John Rushdoony*
>
> *Dr. G. Aiken Taylor*
>
> *Reverend Wilbur G. Williams*

Compiled by Kenneth W. Ingwalson

BETTER BOOKS
PUBLISHER

BOX 2096
Arlington, Virginia 22202

Dedicated to those countless men and women who are rising to defend their Faith, recapture the Protestant Ethic and strengthen Freedom in America.

A Prayer
Instead of a Foreword

WILL NO MAN PLEAD
THY CAUSE?

Oh, gentle Master, where are they
　　Thy friends and all who followed Thee —
The halt, the blind Thy touch restored,
　　The multitudes who called Thee "Lord"?

Scourged, spit upon, with bloody brow,
　　You stand a victim of man's hate;
The mercy man begs Deity,
　　Now man, depraved, denies to Thee.

This judgment hall that reeks with sin
　　Is noxious with the stench of death —
While mad men — Thy accusers — cry
　　"Away with Him!   This man must die."

Again, I ask Thee, where are they
　　Who hailed Thee "Master", "Lord", and "King" —
Where are the hungry folk Ye fed,
　　Who saw Thee touch with life the dead?

Where are Thy 'chosen', Lord, I ask,
　　The Twelve who pledged their love to Thee;
Strong men, they seemed forthright and true —
　　Say not they have forsaken you?

Great God! does no man plead Thy cause,
  Is no voice raised in Thy defense —
Is love men claimed a sham, a fraud,
  A mockery to the living God?

We see Thee led to Calvary today,
  And then complacent go our sinful way —
We close our ears to anguish of Thy cry,
  And by our silence basely Thee deny.

We build proud temples, mutter ancient creeds,
  In liturgy, in orison, we chant and cry,
And as benighted heathen think to win
  Through works — Thy pardon for our grievous sin.

Great God! will we again in this our day,
  When Thou art mocked, forsaken, and alone —
Stand silent and by silence Thee betray,
  While Thou art scourged, condemned, and led away?

Dear God, will no man stand and plead Thy cause,
  Some one Thy hand has touched stand forth for Thee?
Oh, must we hear again Thy anguished cry
  "Why, why, Oh friend, hast thou forsaken me?"

Charles S. Poling

If this volume stirs some to action — help find more men to plead the cause, and break the betrayal of silence, it will have served its mission.

Contents

Kenneth W.
Ingwalson

Introduction

A Layman Looks at

TROUBLE IN THE CHURCHES

Kenneth W. Ingwalson

Publisher, *Human Events;* first Executive Director, Americans for Constitutional Action; former Director, Leadership Services, American Farm Bureau Federation; born in Minnesota and raised in a Lutheran home on a farm in Wisconsin.

Graduated from University of Minnesota and attended its Graduate School and University of Chicago. Held posts as instructor at University of Minnesota, and later Assistant Professor, Rutgers University. Served as County Extension Agent, State Club Agent and State 4-H Club Leader and later worked as Field Agent in the Western States. Was Director of Food, Agriculture and Forestry in Bavaria, Germany, following World War II, with U. S. Military Government.

His work there involved the establishment of improved Agricultural Colleges and schools of Education, the production and distribution of food, fiber and forest products, and the change from centralized control of the economy to a market system and a broad participation of the German people in the affairs of government.

Has been responsible for scores of publications in the fields of youth work, agriculture, leadership training and public policy analysis and development. Co-author of the *ACA Index,* designed to measure the voting behaviour of U. S. Senators and Representatives in respect to upholding Constitutional principles and the Moral Law.

A Layman Looks at

TROUBLE IN THE CHURCHES

by Kenneth W. Ingwalson

Many laymen, clergymen and the press are asking, "What is going on in the Protestant churches?"

One layman visited the Protestant and Orthodox Pavilion of the recent New York World's Fair and viewed the modern motion picture, "The Parable," sponsored by the Protestant Council of New York City. This visit sparked the following letter written to Dr. Dan M. Potter, the Council's Executive Director, in the spring of 1965. It reveals this layman's sense of despair over what is going on in the churches:

Dear Dr. Potter:

While attending the World's Fair last year I sat through an entire performance of "The Parable", and this is what I saw —
— The Holy Land transformed into a circus lot;
— Christ converted into a circus clown, going about "doing good" such as substituting for the boy who was a target for the ball-throwing customers;
— The Crucifixion of Christ caricatured by the clown being strangled by some aerial wires; and
— The Resurrection of Christ caricatured by the clown on his donkey catching up with the circus as it moved out of town.

That is what I saw, as did probably a million or so other people, and if the *Religious News Service* is correct, a million or more people from all over the country will view a performance of this travesty on the life of Christ.

Let's not dignify this sacrilegious display by calling it a parable; let's not degrade His parables by dragging them down to this low level. The implied comparison is extremely odious. Let's characterize it without euphemisms and designate it realistically for what it is — a symbol and symptom of the prostitution and disintegration of Christianity by the very men who are supposedly dedicated and devoted to preaching the Gospel of Christ — not the gospel of a clown.

Recently a good friend of mine sat at lunch with the Dean of the Divinity School of one of the renowned universities in the country. The Dean rejoiced over his student body, containing, as it does, students representing many of the non-Christian religions of the world, the idea being that all of these religions will be poured into a melting pot, out of which will come a brew of a world religion of sorts. Watering down Christianity and substituting some sort of humanistic philosophy.

Over in Brooklyn a minister actively promotes pornographic literature. In San Francisco a group of ministers sponsored a gala dance for homosexuals. Recently in a Manhattan church a couple of dancers displayed their art in the nude. (Such is even banned on Broadway.)

This same Manhattan minister wrote an article calling for a new definition of obscenity, proclaiming that there is nothing obscene in certain 4-letter words which he freely used, and nothing obscene in a picture of specified intimate human relations. I heard not a whimper of protest on any of these matters from the church hierarchy. Who published his article? Union Theological Seminary in its magazine, *Christianity and Crisis.*

This same kind of deterioration is going on in literature, art and music. I am not a theologian, artist or musician — only an interested and deeply concerned observer. But I can claim some degree of knowledge and proficiency in the historical, social, political and economic facts of life, and in any one or all of these capacities I see many threads being woven into a pattern of strange design.

This is what I see:

— The Supreme Court chipping away great chunks from our Constitution and shearing off great reams of our moral fabric;

— the arts being subverted by beatnick-type creators;

— our education system from top to bottom being taken over by Keynesian economists, Fabian Socialists, and a motley crew of "intellectuals" who are ignorant of world history and have no respect for American history and traditions; and

— A church hierarchy that seems to be flushing Christianity down the drain so that the Christian Gospel of salvation may be abandoned in favor of salvation through the passage of welfare state laws.

So I come back to where I started. In this vast pattern of disintegration that is being woven before our eyes, "The Parable," per se, is only a small segment of the whole design. But there it is, and it is a sad commentary on the Protestant Council that it was put there in the first place, and that it is going to be kept there in the second place . . . (signed)

George H. Cless, Jr.
Managing Editor
Christian Economics

But "The Parable" was mild compared with the following lines in a poem written several years ago by Langston Hughes, whose books according to the Methodist Laymen of North Hollywood were on the recommended reading list of the National Council of Churches.[1] He speaks quite clearly:

GOOD-BYE CHRIST

". . . Good-bye.
Christ Jesus Lord God Jehovah,
But beat it on away from here now.
Make way for a new guy with no religion at all —
A real guy named
Marx Communist Lenin Peasant Stalin Worker, ME
I said ME! Go ahead on now,
You're getting in the way of things, Lord.
. . ."

The entire poem is in the same vein!

Protestant church leaders are not as blatant as Hughes but their countless devious and subtle maneuverings as well as the visible actions and open opposition to Christian morals, ethics, standards, and values they sponsor are just as damaging. The end point is the same — destruction of the Christian religion, and with it the American form of constitutional government.

Eleven years ago Milton Mayer, writing in *Motive* magazine, said: "If the Russians conquer America within the next year, they may succeed in saving us from Communism by saving us from celebrating Christmas. The Russians do not believe in God but blasphemy is worse than disbelief. Christmas is a blasphemy . . . . Christmas is a racket, a hissing and abomination." *Motive* is the Methodist Student Movement magazine published monthly by the Division of Higher Education of the Board of Education of the Methodist Church.

Late in 1965 a group of theologians, including Dr. Thomas J. J. Altizer of Emory University, a Methodist institution, proclaimed that "God is dead." This should have shocked every man — Jew or Christian. It did excite some of the alumni to withholding money for its building program. But not *Christian Advocate,* the official organ of the Methodist Church! In its issue of November 18, 1965, it wrote, "Why . . . such a stir when church officials, professors and pastors have known for a number of years that we are in the midst of a theological revolution, in which Altizer plays only one role? (Rev.) Paul Tillich was saying 'God does not exist' three decades ago, and while this is not the same thing as Altizer's 'God is dead,' it still carries the existential stamp which would have the same effect on the average churchgoer if he really heard Tillich."!

No denomination seems to be immune from a godless direct attack of indirect socialist penetration — from inside as well as outside the church.

In the summer of 1965, for instance the Walther League — the young people's organization of the Missouri Lutheran Synod — had Pete Seeger as a featured speaker. Seeger, only a few years ago, invoked the Fifth Amendment before the House Committee on Un-American Activities, rather than deny or confirm that he was a Communist.

In 1963 the same organization featured Dick Gregory. Gregory is the man who, in Bogalusa, Louisiana, reportedly called F.B.I. Director J. Edgar Hoover, "one of the lousiest dogs that ever lived." It seems strange that churches should use this kind of literature and promote these kinds of speakers — even for the stated aim of jolting church members out of their complacency. The means employed are inappropriate to say the least.

Such incidents are not rare or isolated. If these were the only unbelievable "goings on" in the churches, little concern would be expressed. The truth is that these examples are only symptomatic of a movement too widespread to ignore. Its methods are varied, and they express themselves in countless ways. The depth and breadth both of its aims and its consequences are beyond measurement. Yet one thing is certain. It is high time for every Christian to examine what is going on in the Protestant churches, and *why* and *how*, and step up corrective action. It is *Your Church: Their Target*.

While a few conservative Christians have long been concerned with the happenings in their churches, the tendency has been all too often to ignore or dismiss them.

Recently, however, even the liberal, popular press and pulpit have confirmed some of the "goings on", almost with an overture of satisfaction. Wrote, for instance, *Newsweek*, (3 Jan., 1966 issue)" . . .

A passion for a radical transformation of Protestant Christianity in all its contemporary forms and formulas is currently sweeping U.S. churches. To be sure, Protestant churches were filled last week with most of the 68 million Americans who consider themselves Protestants in good standing. The communicants sang the old Christmas hymns, recited familiar creeds, prayed earnestly for "peace on

earth" and admired elaborate creches depicting the birth of
the baby Jesus.

Opposition: But, in the name of the man Jesus, other Prot-
estants this year had defied police barriers to march in
Selma, Ala., paraded before the Pentagon to protest the
Vietnam war, condemned prayers in public schools, rallied
Mexican and Filipino laborers in their strike against
California fruit growers and joined Roman Catholics in
celebrating Mass. And a few theologians — again in Jesus's
name — even exulted in the "death of God." . . ."

The effects of the de-Christianizing movements
are widespread. Often the results seem far removed from the churches.

Atheistic ideology at the most, and doubt about
deep religious principles at the least, are widespread. Atheistic existentialism has a wide following and may be providing an intellectual substitute for faith in God and for His immutable
moral law.

It seems obvious that doubt about Christian
values and religious truths is actually being
taught in our Protestant churches and educational
institutions. If doubt stems from ignorance, such
ignorance is not being dispelled. How can it be if
the study of the Bible proceeds from the thesis
that it is a collection of myths and not the true
Word of God? Absence of Christian faith and
knowledge can hardly be blamed on the student.
In his idealistic period of his life, at a time when
the world seems all in change, when he is
searching somehow for the meaning of life, for
strong stays to grasp and something stable on
which to lean, many churches and preachers are
spreading doubt and associating themselves with
secular systems that have no stability.

Recently my wife and I were godparents at an
infant baptism. Before the ceremony, the meaning of the sacrament was explained in a brief-
ing session for all participants. Referring to

the Ten Commandments and other Scriptural
texts, the pastor said: "These, of course, are
only symbols — stories in the Bible — from
which we may each take our own meaning." Not
the Word of God! Not immutable laws which we
violate at our peril! And the pastor is from the
pulpit of one of the oldest and most famous
churches in America.

Whence comes this lack of knowledge, lack of
faith, lack of belief in eternal verities? How is
it fostered? What *is* going on in the Christian
churches today?

There are those who believe that the "goings
on" in the churches, the disbelief in Christian
truths and the growth of the "new morality" are
a result of the increase in scientific knowledge —
or, at least, the employment of the scientific
method of reasoning. Since science explains so
many former mysteries and the scientific method
questions all assertions, there no longer seems
to be a dividing line between the secular and the
sacred.

Yet some top scientists disagree.

Werner von Braun, the space scientist, reflects
the view of a great number of his colleagues when
he says "Science may not have a moral dimension. But I am certain that science in its search
for new insights into the nature of creation has
produced new ethical values of its own. Most
certainly science has fostered veracity and
humility." Then he continues: "The materialists
of the nineteenth century and their Marxist heirs
of the twentieth, tried to tell us that, as science
gives us more knowledge about the creation, we
could live without faith in a Creator. Yet so far,
with every new answer, we have discovered new
questions. The better we understand the intri-
cacies of the atomic structure, the nature of life,

or the master plan for the galaxies, the more reason we have found to marvel at the wonder of God's creation. But our need for God is not based on awe alone. Man needs faith just as he needs food, water or air. With all the science in the world, we need faith in God, whenever faith in ourselves has reached its limit." [2]

Perhaps the phenomena of "what's going on in the churches" can be attributed to the new role that some of the clergy are assuming. They seem no longer to have faith in prayer or to believe that God works his wonders through individuals. No longer do they hold to the Biblical strategy for accomplishment, "Not by might, nor by power, but by my Spirit, saith the Lord of Hosts" (Zechariah 4:6) Large numbers of clergy in every denomination seem to feel that such a process is too slow for society and not rewarding enough for him. They have to be in Berkeley, Selma, the White House, Chicago or Harlem acting for God and getting in the headlines. These "men of the cloth" take to political issues, meddle in secular matters and venture beyond their competence in economic affairs. They seem hardly to understand the consequences of this sort of social action. These social reformers see no connection between professed "non-violent civil disobedience" in Washington in May, 1964 and the riots in Los Angeles in August, 1965 resulting in at least 34 deaths and over $100 million damage, or the vandalism on the last day of the New York World's Fair. Apparently they see nothing wrong in the use of $40,000 of taxpayers money to produce a foul, racist and pornographic-laden play in New York. No cry of anguish arises from them when Playwright Le Roi Jones was reported by the *Associated Press* in mid-November, 1965 as saying, "I don't see anything wrong with hating white people."

In hundreds of instances congregations are being rent asunder by politically-minded preachers. After all, in secular matters, be they political, business, economic or social, intelligent members of the congregation have their own views, experience, and competence. They are not about to accept the theory that the preacher has a "pipeline to the Almighty" on these matters. And if he hasn't, the layman reasons, how do I know that he is not a fraud in spiritual matters as well.

And while many clergymen, goaded on by the left-leaning hierarchy, are promoting a socialist economy, they fail to see its utter failure. Unlearned in sound economics, they hardly recognize the virtues in a competitive market system. Currenly the liberal left are among those calling for America to feed the starving people of the whole world. They might wisely consider the words of one of our nations' greatest food and agricultural experts — Charles B. Shuman, President of the American Farm Bureau Federation. He pointed out on December 13, 1965 "that socialism must be blamed for world hunger because it is the one common denominator that applies to nearly all hungry nations."

Confusing at least is the spectacle of clergymen marching against the law or asserting that man has the duty to disobey any law his conscience tells him is unjust. Laymen are skeptical that a marching horde of 5,000 or 10,000 emotionally motivated people can reach a sensible conclusion simultaneously! Clerical participation in matters of government policy, administration, appointments of officials, and public school programs does not square with the citizen's concept of "separation of Church and State." They wonder

"from whence comes the signal for such pronouncements or radical behavior?" From God?
Or from some subversive source?

Some clergymen have become involved inno-
cently, naively or otherwise in strictly partisan
political programs. They promote the war on
poverty, urban renewal, medicare and federal
aids for all conceivable problems. In Cleveland,
for instance, a voter registration drive was conducted with a $20,000 grant from the National
Council of Churches. Did members of Council-
affiliated churches expect that their contributions
would be used for such political purposes? Or to
invoke the coercive power of government? Little
do church leaders realize the hard political facts
of life and that most of such projects are motivated by the votes they will secure for some
political party or officeholder — not by the
Christian love it will or will not inspire. But it
is precisely at this point that denominational
church hierarchies are "fanning the flames" that
may well be destructive of true Christianity.

Nearly every denomination has set up some
kind of social action unit, most of them encouraged and blueprinted with the help of the National Council of Churches. Soon all become
possessed with the search for power. And this
power they have come to realize is achieved
through the political process. They meet in groups
and enlist political leaders to learn how to convert other clergymen to support government-
sponsored programs. They sign and circulate
petitions ranging all the way from clamoring for
government housing programs to capitulating to
the Communists in Viet Nam or elsewhere on
any terms, apparently.

Lobby offices for a dozen or more denominations are now located and active in Washington,

D.C. The National Council of Churches has a legislative lobby office, as do the Roman Catholics. So does the Friends' Committee on National Legislation. While most of them reject the idea of being lobbyists, yet when leftist causes or legislation comes along, most seem to suddenly preach and propagandize the same party line. Among such programs are: the abolition of the House Committee on Un-American Activities, supporting proposed repeal of 14(b) in the Taft-Hartley Act, advocating disarmament of the United States and the admission of Red China to the United Nations.

Yet while speaking, petitioning, playwriting and printing on all kinds of secular or political issues, opposition to godless communism is seldom urged by the same actionists. Dr. Frederick Brown Harris, Chaplain of the U.S. Senate, commenting on this odd phenomena, says; ". . . But with this menace (the godless Communist system) hanging like a Damoclean sword over the fragile thread of our liberties, are these same religious leaders so vociferous now as they deal with growing pains of a democracy, equally vocal as they face the most dastardly system the ages have known? It is a tragic fact that the answer to that question must be no! Among those who are assuming national and world leadership among the churches, it must be admitted that so far as communism is concerned, there is, to use a Scriptural phrase, 'a silence that could be heard in Heaven'."

Granted, not all clergymen follow these nudgings on behalf of secular projects. How many is hard to say. Yet it is encouraging to note that one Minister at least found it desirable to write a 6000 word "white paper" to members of his congregation, that "bucks the tide."

On Dec. 9, 1965, the Reverend Dr. George R.
Davis of the National City Christian Church of
Washington, D. C., wrote: . . .

"The National City Christian Church has made
remarkable strides," the paper said. "Our membership includes Japanese, Chinese, Korean,
Latin American, Negro and others. The projects
we sponsor are far reaching in our neighbor-
hood. People of all races and nationalities worship with us regularly, as well as all creeds and
denominations, and religions. Our doors are wide
open to all."

"But we do not crusade, we do not bellow,
we do not march, we do not demonstrate," Davis
wrote. "At least your senior minister doesn't.
We do not join every cause, promote every
issue, get involved in every pressure group
demand. We do move forward. We do make
progress. We are a church. And I do not believe
at all that the only test of a 'relevant church'
is in crusading."

Then he continued that a White House conference condemning the report on Negro family
life made by Daniel Moynihan showed further
evidence that "some conferences do not look for
truth, they look for dogmatisms."

An increasing number of church members are
becoming aware of something alien going on in
the churches. Some churches and leaders are
doing something about it. Yet, the truth is — the
enemy of the Protestant ethic is well entrenched.
To dislodge him will not be easy. The leaders of
the "new morality" are on the march.

One of the vehicles of the radical leftists is
the civil rights movement and the so-called non-
violent civil disobedience technique. Training
schools for ministers are being set up and conducted by professional radicals. In July, 1965,

fifty Episcopalians spent three weeks in inten-
sive training in Claremont, California, under a
Saul Alinsky. In August, fifty Presbyterian min-
isters in northern California took the course.
Alinsky's plans called for similar seminars in
Rochester, N. Y., Detroit, Buffalo and Kansas
City. Although he is a Jew, no Jewish rabbis take
part in his training — only Protestant and Roman
Catholic clerics. The training? One topic is: *How
to upset the community power structure.* (By
Christian love? Oh, no, he says, goad them, con-
fuse them, irritate them and most of all make
them live by their own rules!) Another topic is:
*How to take from the haves and give it to the
have nots.* (Alinsky's salary is reported to be
$25,000). Does he come in uninvited? Indeed not.
The communities raise up to $100,000 for his
invasion.

Doesn't it seem strange that churches have
difficulty in raising funds to carry on their ministry, yet programs of this sort can command
support of this magnitude? Can it be that the
churches are being used as a vehicle to help
socialize America? Or, is it that the churches,
deserting the Scriptures as divine truth, deny-
ing the existence of moral absolutes, and concerning themselves with shaping the form of
society rather than stressing the transformation
of individuals, are substituting government for
God?

Consider the following by the Rev. John F. E.
Green, D. C. of McKeesport, Pa: "The early
church lived and flourished in the warfare against
the anti-Christ. Warfare demands dedication, even
unto loss of life. All the apostles died as martyrs
— witnesses to the Christ, to the infinite value of
their own soul, greater than the satisfaction of
the wants of the social animal. The entire book of

the Apocalypse is a <u>paean of defiance of</u> the anti-
Christ and a trumpet-call to warfare against him,
with the prospect that evil will win the first
battle, but that God will restore his reign in a
new heaven and a new earth.

A spokesman for the present world of atheist
socialism, the ground-plan of Communism states
this very plainly and frankly. In the boldness of
the advocates of the 'brave new world,' of
Socialist-Communism, he says "We Socialists of
the ADA (Americans for Democratic Action)
believe in man as a social animal and not in a
God who does not exist; or who, if He exists,
is irrelevant. We believe, as does Arthur Schle-
singer, Jr. major author of the Democratic
platform of 1960 and 1964, that government
exists to satisfy the needs of man as a social
animal, and its function is to build a heaven
here on earth through socialism and not to be
concerned with some mythical hereafter . . .
This will free man. Instead of looking to a
heaven based on a nonexistent God, he will be
thankful that he has a heaven here on earth . . .
After paying his taxes, he is free from worry,
want or responsibilities, to lead a happy and
creative life."[3]

To many ministers and laymen loyal to their
Christian beliefs, the object of what is happening
in and out of many churches is clear. For instance, the Rev. Kenneth W. Sollitt, of the First
Baptist Church of Midland, Mich., expresses it as
follows:

If I Were The Devil

If I wanted to turn America into a Communist hell, I think
I would do something like this:

I would cultivate among the people the idea that the individual
is nothing the indiscriminate mass of people everything. I

would also seek to convince Americans that God and Christian ethics and an honest desire to make one's way in the
world are old-fashioned.

I would get elected to office on the promise of helping everybody at someone else's expense.

Then, I'd treat the Constitution as a sort of handbook on the
philosophy of government to be referred to only if it served
my purpose.

I would increase the size and scope of government in every
way possible, going into every conceivable business in competition with established enterprises, paying the state's business losses out of the treasury. I would try to keep hidden
how this could lead at the right time to the nationalization of
industry.

I would thus create a government strong enough to give its
citizens everything they wanted. Thus, I could create a
government strong enough to take from them everything they
have.

By combination of inflation and taxes, I would rob the very
people I pretend to help until, if they ever should want to
return to freedom, they couldn't — but would be dependent
on the state.

Next, I would gradually raise taxes to 100 per cent of income
(we are one third of the way now) so that the state could have
it all. Then I'd give back to the people enough to keep them
alive and little enough to keep them enslaved.

In the meantime, I would take from those who have and give
to those who want until I killed the incentive of the presently
ambitious man and satisfied the meager needs of the rest.
The police state would then be required to make everybody
work — and the transformation of America from a republic
to a second rate Communist nation would be complete.

Do you see in this similarities to what we have been doing
for 30 years? 4

Christians of all faiths are disturbed. They are
asking: "What shall we do?"

This book is addressed to them.

It seems prudent to first take a look at what is
actually going on in the churches.

Some activities are open and flagrant, like the
use of left-wing folksingers, or the pronounce-

ment of political positions seeming to commit the churches as a whole, or the endorsement of the "jungle" principle "each his own judge of law."

Other goings on are quite invisible to the layman. What about behind-the-scenes writing of "position papers," advanced by the "hierarchy" as good gospel; or the gradual acceptance of the government's role in the affairs of charity or missions; the training of young ministers for the questionable role of advocating programs consistent with communist or socialist goals; the use of methods that create doubt or deny Christian truths. The very foundations of America are at stake!

Dr. Charles S. Poling, whose stirring message you will find in this book, said on August 15, 1965, "Can the church long survive in a socialist communist state? I have dedicated these latter days of my life to challenge Christians and the church we love to get back to being the church. The church as a political arm cannot save the Republic, but the church returning to her Pilgrim character and functioning as the church of the Living God, making evil men good and leading the lost to the cleansing of the redemptive cross, can still save society, our nation, and our free way of life.

Before Union Theological Seminary of New York became captured by the socialist liberals, Union's professor of Church History was the great and good Philip Schaff. I quote from this noble Christian patriot. He wrote 'Republican institutions in the hands of a virtuous and God-fearing nation are the very best in the world, but in the hands of corrupt and irreligious people they are the very worst, and the most effective weapon of destruction. An indignant people may rise in rebellion against a cruel tyrant; but who

will rise against the tyranny of the people in possession of the ballot-box and the whole machinery of government? Here lies our great danger, and it is increasing every year. Destroy our churches, close our Sunday-Schools, abolish the Lord's Day, and our republic would become an empty shell, and our people would tend to heathenism and barbarism. Christianity is the most powerful factor in our society and the pillar of our institutions. It regulates the family; it enjoins private and public virtue; it builds up moral character; it teaches us to love God supremely, and our neighbor as ourselves; it makes good men and useful citizens; it denounces every vice; it encourages every virtue; it promotes and serves the public welfare; it upholds peace and order. Christianity is the only possible religion for the American people, and with Christianity are bound up all our hopes for the future.'
(Phillip Schaff 1888)

The "Huns and Vandals" Macaulay so accurately prophesied are here; they have taken over our institutions of higher learning and theological seminaries; they stalk through our halls of government, and have become overlords in our liberal socialist pulpits. The portrait Philip Schaff presents of the true church is a far cry from the political religious machine carrying the banner of the church today."

Perhaps you and every concerned Christian must first realize that "Your church is their target."

For these and many other reasons this book has been created. Here between its covers are the distilled thoughts of thirteen men, from several different denominations, representing several theological traditions, but all concerned with "What's going on in the Protestant churches today?".

Each is competent in his own field and each brings well-documented descriptions about what is going on, how it started, how it is being carried out, who is involved, and why the end point leads us to a kind of religion and a form of society that man has tried to escape since the beginning of time.

To each of these writers, every Christian who reads this book owes a debt of gratitude. For each in his own way has highlighted the problems at hand in a constructive and responsible manner. They have not been paid to write their chapter. Each has expressed his convictions in the hopes that his contribution would aid in the salvation of the Protestant ethic.

These men may not always agree with each other on details. Neither will you agree with all they say. But the problem and challenge for laymen and clergymen has been made crystal clear.

To my personal friends, the Rev. Irving E. Howard and the Rev. Edmund A. Opitz, a special word of gratitude is due. In addition to writing two original and extremely relevant chapters these men helped delineate the various aspects of the problem and made it possible to find this panel of contributors of extraordinary competence.

With the evidence here compiled and suggestions offered you should be prepared, with your Bible, to join a crusade to correct the evils. The starting point for action is in your own heart — your own church — your own pulpit — your own Sunday School — your own community. America may yet come out of this crisis stronger, if you do.

"Be ready always to give an answer to every man that asketh you a reason for the hope that is in you." (1 Peter 3:15)

Irving E.
Howard

Chapter 1

Who did it - and How

PROTESTANT PROPHETS
OF COLLECTIVISM

IRVING E. HOWARD

Irving E. Howard graduated from Gordon College in 1937, and from Gordon Divinity School in 1940. He is a member of Gordon's honorary society, Phi Alpha Chi.

Later he received an S.T.B. from Harvard, an M.A. in history and international relations from Clark University, Worcester, Massachusetts, and an M.B.A. from the Graduate School of Business Administration, New York University.

After having been pastor of three churches in Massachusetts, in September 1954, he left the pulpit of Hope Congregational Church, Worcester, Massachusetts, to join the staff of the Christian Freedom Foundation, New York City, as Assistant Editor of *Christian Economics*.

As a member of Christian Freedom Foundation, he has been speaking before church and business groups and writing for its publication. His articles have appeared in *Human Events* and other magazines, and he has won four Freedom Foundation Awards for published material.

Mr. Howard has also served as a lecturer in Friend's University, Wichita, Kansas; McKendree College, Lebanon, Illinois; Northwest Christian College, Eugene, Oregon and other schools.

Who did it - and How

PROTESTANT PROPHETS
OF COLLECTIVISM

by Irving E. Howard

"What on Earth is Happening to Protestant-ism?" was asked by Duncan Norton-Taylor in the December, 1965, issue of *Fortune.* What is happening to Protestantism is but a part of what is happening to western civilization. Both are under attack by enemies bent on their de-struction. Sadly, however, Protestantism is also destroying itself.

Out of personal tragedy Whittaker Chambers came to an understanding of the issue facing the West: "The crisis of the Western world exists to the degree in which the Western world actually shares Communism's materialist vision, is so dazzled by the logic of the materialist interpreta-tion of history, politics, and economics, that it fails to grasp that, for it, the only possible an-swer to the Communist challenge: Faith in God or Faith in Man? is the challenge: Faith in God." [1]

The Protestant prophets of collectivism have — wittingly or unwittingly — affirmed Faith in Man. True to Whittaker Chambers' analysis, this Faith in Man has been driving inexorably toward com-munism — or its equivalent.

Just how far the clergy themselves have moved in this direction was revealed by a scientific sur-vey conducted by the Opinion Research Corpora-tion in 1960. *Christianity Today* reported the results of this survey: "The pollsters designated

two percent of the ministers as communist, ten
percent as socialist and fifteen percent as fellow-
travelers in their economic outlook."[2] To be
sure, the vast majority of ministers are conservative in their economic outlook, but Socialists are in places of influence in the various denominational structures. For example, Dr. John
A. Mackay, former president of Princeton Theological Seminary, former president of the World
Presbyterian Alliance, former moderator of the
General Assembly of the Presbyterian Church,
U.S.A., and presently a member of the central
committee of the World Council of Churches,
said in 1961: "It is evident that Marxist communism has certain affinities with Christianity,
— for example, in its criticism of the capitalist
system, its passion for social justice, and its
aspirations for a better world."[3]

How did we get this way?

It is a long story that reaches back to the latter decades of the nineteenth century — and beyond, if one wishes to pursue the trail.

I. Fabian Socialism

The collectivist propaganda in Protestantism
acquired the name "Social Gospel" during the
early decades of the twentieth century and, since
the 1930's, has continued as "Social Action."
Whatever the name, the collectivist movement in
Protestantism has passed through three clearly
defined stages since the 1880's: Fabian socialism, Marxian socialism, and Keynesian socialism. As always in history, there has been much
overlapping.

Richard T. Ely

One root of the Social Gospel in American
Protestantism can be traced to a college pro-

fessor, Richard T. Ely, who ended his days a conservative economist. During the years he was most influential with Protestant ministers, however, he was a Fabian Socialist.

Ely was one of the first American economists with a German doctorate. After graduating from Columbia University in 1876, he studied economics at the University of Heidelberg where the Old Historical School of Economics was the fad of the hour with Karl Knies as its leading light.

He and the other members of the Old Historical School were disciples of that greater name in nineteenth century Germany — Hegel. Hegelianism denied all absolutes except reason which Hegel believed was personified in man. The goal of the historical process, according to Hegelianism, is the State. In fact, Hegel almost deified the State.

It is not surprising that the Old Historical School, under the influence of Hegelianism, gave a large place to government.

Moreover, Karl Knies and his colleagues rejected the classical concept of fixed economic laws. They rejected the belief that man is motivated by self-interest. They affirmed an altruism which looked like Christianity to Richard T. Ely, but was merely a sentimental humanism. Karl Knies talked of the ethical basis of economics, but it was ethics divorced from the Christian doctrine of sin and therefore without realism regarding human nature.

Richard T. Ely accepted the point of view of Karl Knies enthusiastically and uncritically. Later in life he said: "If I did have any Bible, it would be found in the books and lectures of Professor Karl Knies." [4]

After graduating from the University of

Heidelberg, Ely spent a year in Berlin studying Bismark's welfare state, noting many of its features with approval. On his return trip to America, he visited the Fabian Socialists in London, England. For many years after this visit, he corresponded with Sidney and Beatrice Webb and Edward R. Pease.

The Fabians were committed to a policy of gradualism rather than revolution and this appealed to Ely. Imitating the great Roman General from whom they took their name, the Fabians studiously avoided any direct conflict with capitalism while they sought to undermine the capitalistic system by maneuvering their men into key positions in journalism, education, and the professions.

The June 1892 issue of the *Fabian News* described their method: "A cover of respectability and good manners as a means of gaining entry into all social activities, while avoiding the use of the label 'socialism', promoting socialism continuously by coloring such activities with new terms so as to attain socialism by stealth."[5]

One year after returning to America from Germany, Ely joined the staff of Johns Hopkins University. Here he taught such famous leaders as Woodrow Wilson, John R. Commons, Senator La Follette, and others; wrote many books and magazine articles, and engineered the organization of the American Economic Association.

Although quite unorthodox in his theology, Ely was an evangelist turned economist. All of his books had a religious flavor and two of them, *The Social Aspects of Christianity* (1889), and *The Social Law of Service* (1896), were written specifically for ministers and Christian laymen.

In these, Ely bluntly revealed his reason for concentrating upon the churches: "The most pow-

why is the Church a target for sinful men?

erful social force known to man is religion; beyond anything else, it has shaped and is shaping the world's history."[6]

Both of these books were expositions of a sentimental humanism. Ely said: "This I regard as the grand distinctive feature of Christianity, the exaltation of humanity."[7]

Ely's doctrine of the State was most alarming of all. He described the State as a "continuous, conscious organism, and a moral personality"[8] even ascribing divinity to it: "Christ and His apostles always recognized the authority of the State as divine in character even under most trying and perplexing circumstances."[9] Ely carried his theory of the State to the point of giving it power to change human nature. One of his chapters was: "Making Men Good By Law." [10]

In 1892, Ely moved to the University of Wisconsin where he was accused of teaching socialism by someone outside the University. The University appointed a committee to investigate Ely, conducted a trial, and acquitted the professor of the charges. However, Joseph Dorfman, about sixty years later in *The Economic Mind in American Civilization* (1959) sided with Ely's accuser and described Ely as a "Christian Socialist." [11] He might as well have called him a Fabian Socialist for, during his earlier years, Ely openly admired the Fabians and recommended their policies of indirection and gradualism.

During his Wisconsin years, Ely was influenced by the Austrian School of Economics. Eventually he turned from socialism and became the author of one of the most popular textbooks on economics, *Outlines of Economics*. Richard T. Ely died October 4, 1943, at Old Lyme, Connecticut allegedly regretting his earlier social-

opened eyes too late b

istic activity. But it was too late to negate the influence he had had during his Fabian years. Unfortunately, he shaped the thinking of many Protestant ministers, the most famous being Washington Gladden.

Washington Gladden

A New England Puritan never forgot the theocracy. Even when the idea was no longer in his conscious mind, the memory of the day when the churches ran society (even to fixing prices) lay in his subconscious, whetting his appetite for a return to such secular power. Like Richard T. Ely, Washington Gladden was of New England Puritan ancestory with this memory of theocracy.

While minister of the First Congregational Church of North Adams, Massachusetts, Gladden distinguished himself by defending Horace Bushnell. The orthodox Congregational clergy looked upon Bushnell as a dangerous heretic and tongues must have wagged when Gladden invited Bushnell to preach his installation sermon.

Most Congregationalists of that period objected to two items in Bushnell's thought. First, Bushnell reduced the crucifixion of Christ to a humanistic example of self-sacrifice. His other controversial doctrine was spelled out in his famous book, *Christian Nurture* (1847). In this he declared that if children were reared in a Christian environment, they would not need to be converted by evangelism.

While this environmentalism seems harmless at first glance, Gladden made it the basis of what came to be known as the Social Gospel. At the heart of that "Gospel" was the conviction that a good environment will make good citizens. The idea still lingers in much modern welfare state legislation.

In 1875, Gladden became minister of the North Congregational Church of Springfield, Massachusetts. Here he produced one of the earliest tracts of the Social Gospel, the *Workingmen and their Employers* (1876). This consisted of a series of Sunday evening lectures on the relations between labor and management which he had delivered during the first year of his pastorate. Thirty-seven years later, in his *Recollections,* Gladden said that *Workingmen and their Employers* was "not quite so sympathetic as it ought to have been" toward labor unions.[12] The fact is, Gladden had grown much more sympathetic toward socialism during the interim.

Up to this time, Washington Gladden was only a voice crying in western Massachusetts. Then a call came from the First Congregational Church of Columbus, Ohio, and Gladden and his family moved to this new charge during the Christmas week of 1882. While in this pastorate he became a national figure.

In 1885, the Reverend Josiah Strong invited him to an "Inter-Denominational Congress" meeting in his church in Cincinnati together with Lyman Abbott, Richard T. Ely and Amory Bradford to discuss social problems. If this was the first time Gladden met Richard T. Ely, it was not the last. This same year, Ely took his first steps toward forming the American Economic Association calling upon Washington Gladden and Lyman Abbott to assist him. Gladden's friendship continued to deepen over the years.

In the same year as the Saratoga Conference at which Gladden helped to organize the American Economic Association, he also addressed the National Council of Congregational Churches at Worcester, Massachusetts on "Christian Socialism." In answer to the question: "Is Christianity

in any sense socialistic?" Gladden echoed Ely
when he said: "It begins to be clear that Christianity is not individualism. The Christian religion has encountered no deadlier foe during the
last century than that individualistic philosophy
which underlies the competitive system." [13]

Shortly after this, Gladden gave another series
of Sunday evening lectures in his church on social questions. They were published in 1887 with
the title: *Applied Christianity.* In this he said
that socialism's indictment of modern society
described "the natural issues of an industrial
system whose sole motive power is self-interest,
and whose sole regulative principle is competition." [14]

The turmoil of the following years seemed to
support Gladden's contention that the social system was wrong. There were strikes and rioting
in 1892 in Idaho; at Homestead, Pennsylvania in
the steel mills and in the coal mines in west
Tennessee. 1893 brought a financial panic. 1894
saw a great coal strike and Coxey's army of
unemployed marching on Washington and also the
Pullman strike and the American Railway Union
strike. The 1890's were not gay. They were
worse than the 1880's, but America was only
suffering the pains associated with economic
growth.

To Washington Gladden it seemed as if society
were flying apart. Looking for a remedy, he persuaded the National Council of Congregational
Churches to organize a Committee of Five on
Labor and Capital, marking the beginning of a
social action movement in Congregationalism.

When Gladden wrote *Social Facts and Forces*
in 1897, the unification of society was uppermost
in his mind. His Puritan ancestors had believed
that the sovereignty of God served this purpose

rather well, but Gladden had long since rejected that doctrine, so he turned to the State. The State should be the unifying agent, he thought, but he found that it could not unify society because too many people, in his opinion, had the wrong idea of its function. He wrote: "Let me say again that this conception of the State, that it is merely a police force, is, to my mind, a wholly erroneous conception; that the State is something far higher and more godlike than this and that if we could only invest it in our thought with its true divine character, we should need no other agency for the unification of society." [15]

He then turned to the churches, but found them not equipped for the task. This, however, he felt could be remedied. The churches could be brought together and made into a political force and thus become the cement of society.

Gladden was an activist. Once persuaded of something he took steps to do it. He helped engineer the first plan of a merger of the Congregational Churches with the Christian Churches. Although this merger was not consummated until 1931, Washington Gladden and others started the proceedings in the 1890's.

Gladden pioneered in many other ecumenical explorations before the twentieth century, and when the Federal Council of Churches was organized in 1908, it was in a very real sense a fulfillment of Gladden's dream of an organization through which the churches could unite for political action.

Gladden's anti-capitalistic bias was always just beneath the surface of his thought. In 1905, while he was moderator of the National Council of Congregational Churches, Gladden startled the Congregationalists by publicly protesting the acceptance by that denomination's foreign mission

board of a gift of $100,000 from John D. Rocke-
feller. His paper was entitled: "Shall Ill-Gotten
Gains Be Sought for Christian Purposes?"

Washington Gladden never understood the factors necessary for economic growth nor the contribution capitalism had made, and has continued
to make, to the welfare of all classes in American
society — an understanding which marked the
latter years of Professor Ely's career.

In 1918, while World War I was entering its
final phase, Washington Gladden died. He left
behind two monuments to his reforming zeal:
the Social Gospel in American Protestantism and
the movement within the Protestant Churches toward united political action.

Walter Rauschenbusch

The American dislocations following the Civil
War also left their mark on a young German
Baptist minister who was serving the Second
Baptist Church in West Forty-Fifth Street, New
York City. In later years, this minister, Walter
Rauschenbusch, writing of his New York pastor-
ate recalled ". . . the procession of men out of
work, out of clothes, out of shoes, and out of
hope. They wore down our threshold and they
wore out our hearts." [16]

Walter Rauschenbusch was to become the most
scholarly and the most persuasive representative
of the social gospel movement in America. He
was born in the opening year of the Civil War,
1861, in Rochester, New York. His father, Augustus Rauschenbusch, had been of German Lutheran lineage, but when Augustus migrated from
Ontario, Canada to Rochester, New York, he was
a Baptist minister.

Walter was educated in Germany and the University of Rochester. He graduated from Ro-

chester Theological Seminary in 1886 and his
New York pastorate followed. During the earliest
phase of this ministry, his reading concentrated
on the usual fare of a minister, theology and
devotional material, but his biographer, Vernon
Bodein, discovered that in 1890 there was a
marked shift to literature on social questions.
Included among this later reading was the address of Richard T. Ely of Johns Hopkins University, "Natural Monopolies and Local Taxation."[17]

Professor Richard T. Ely continued to be one
of his guiding lights. Other authors in his early
reading list were Ruskin, F. D. Maurice, Robert-
son of Brighton, Tolstoi, Karl Marx, Mazzini,
Bellamy, J. S. Mill and Henry George, who was
particularly important to him. In 1886, he enthusiastically supported Henry George for mayor of
New York City. George was defeated in his candi-
dacy, but he won Rauschenbusch as a disciple.
Walter Rauschenbusch later confessed that this
reformer first awakened him to the world of
social problems.

Three years after the defeat of Henry George,
Walter Rauschenbusch joined with Leighton Williams, Elizabeth Post, and J. E. Raymond to publish a radical monthly periodical entitled *For the
Right*. Rauschenbusch was its editor.

His radical editorship of *For the Right* was
interrupted in 1891 by a year of study in Germany. Enroute he stopped off in England and
explored Birmingham, Liverpool, and London.
During this visit, like Richard T. Ely before him,
he became acquainted with the Fabian Socialists
with whom he continued to have contact during
the following years.

As Ely found his mentor in Karl Knies, Walter
Rauschenbusch found his in the thought of Al-

brecht Ritschl, the neo-Kantian professor of systematic theology at Bonn and Gottingen who had
died a few years before Rauschenbusch's arrival.
Ritschl's theology was still dominant in the theological circles of Germany. In keeping with the
trend in Germany during his life, Ritschl had
shifted the emphasis from the individual to the
community. "Moral collectivism" is a phrase
that has been applied to Ritschlianism. Consequently, Rauschenbusch returned to America
confirmed in his collectivist, pragmatic interpretation of the Gospel.

Walter Rauschenbusch was a minor voice in
America until 1897, when he accepted a post as
teacher of New Testament at Rochester Theological Seminary. In 1902, he moved to the
chair of Church History. Thus, Rauschenbusch
was able to mold the theological students who
for over fifteen years passed through his class-
rooms.

At first, the professor was too busy to try to
reform the world, but by 1901 he was address-
ing the Labor Lyceum of Rochester, New York
on "Dogmatic and Practical Socialism." In 1907,
before leaving for a third period of study in
Germany, he finished the manuscript of *Christianity and the Social Crisis*. When he returned
from Europe, he found himself famous. This
book sold over fifty thousand copies.

Christianity and the Social Crisis was a devastating criticism of modern society and a
plea for the application of Christianity to its
problems — by which Rauschenbusch meant
Christian socialism. At any rate, the Socialists
who read his book understood him to mean that.
Soon after its publication, a leader of the Socialist Party called on Rauschenbusch and invited him to join that Party. The reforming

professor refused. Following Fabian tactics, he never indentified himself with the Socialist Party.

Yet, in 1909, he wrote an article for *The Call* (January 28, 1909): "Socialism is Coming." There is no doubt that he was convinced of the inevitability of socialism, although he never clearly defined what he meant by the term.

By the first decade of the twentieth century, Rauschenbusch had gained a national reputation as a social reformer. In 1911, he was invited to give the Earl Lectures at the Pacific Theological Seminary in Berkeley, California, and in 1911, the Merrick Lectures at Ohio Wesleyan University, Delaware, Ohio. In these two lecturships, he tried to answer the question: "How can you do it?" These lectures formed the nucleus of his how-to-do-it book published in 1912, *Christianizing the Social Order*.

In this, his most radical work, he pilloried capitalism as a "wicked system" and saw two forces working toward the transformation of this "wicked system" into a cooperative commonwealth — trade unionism and socialism. He admitted that socialism would abolish the present system, while the trade unions working from within sought only to remedy the so-called abuses within the capitalist structure. In this book, at least, Rauschenbusch clearly leaned toward the socialist remedy. In fact, he rejected Professor Ely's concession that socialism is inefficient and predicted that socialism would lead the world to greater efficiency.[18] Although Rauschenbusch was never a Marxist and refused to join the Socialist Party, he moved much farther to the left than either Ely or Gladden.

He moved others to the left also. Norman Thomas, a former minister and many times Socialist candidate for president wrote to Dr. V.

Raymond Edman, former president of Wheaton
College: "The writings of the Baptist clergyman,
Walter Rauschenbusch, had more to do with
making me a Socialist than anything which I read
in Marx. Indeed, I became a Socialist because it
seemed to me that democratic socialism was the
best interpretation of the Christian ethic which
I could find for our time." [19]

By the time Walter Rauschenbusch wrote his
last book, World War I was well on its way and
the United States was poised to invade Europe
to defeat Germany. Rauschenbusch was of German
descent. In the October 15, 1914 issue of *The
Congregationalist,* Rauschenbusch had written an
article, "Be Fair to Germany: a Plea for Open
Mindedness." He found that few were open
minded, and that even old friends were suspicious
of him because he refused to condemn the "Hun."

When he went to Yale to deliver the Taylor
Lectures in 1917, it was with a heavy heart. The
lectures were later published as *A Theology for
the Social Gospel.* This book was much more restrained than his former ones. It marked his
first use of the term "Social Gospel" and a
studious avoidance of the world "socialism."

Restrained or not, his bitterness toward capitalism remained. In this last book, he made the
much quoted statement that God is against capitalism. [20]

In theology, this book revealed a continued
drift toward humanism. Rauschenbusch rejected
the transcendence of God and described God as
immanent in humanity. He defined man's con-
sciousness of God as the counterpart of his con-
sciousness of his followmen. [21] Visser 't Hooft
writing of this tendency said: "The idea of a
democratic God indicates very clearly that the
direction of thought of the social gospel is to-

ward pantheism. Even as in a democratic state the government is merely the expression of the will of the people, just so God stands for the totality of the strivings of humanity." [22]

Thus, Walter Rauschenbusch ended his career asserting Faith in Man.

II. Marxian Socialism

The Social Gospel of Walter Rauschenbusch suffered a mortal wound in the blood bath of World War I. The War was followed by a temporary reaction against socialism. Consequently, very few of the organizations created by the Social Gospel survived the twenties. Those that did included the Methodist Federation for Social Service organized in 1907; the Episcopal Church Association for the Advancement of the Interests of Labor which became the Episcopal Department of Christian Social Service in 1926; and the Church League for Industrial Democracy which in 1919 developed out of the Church Socialist League. The most important offspring of the Social Gospel, the Federal Council of Churches, weathered a heavy barrage of criticism during the twenties and survived to become the politically powerful National Council of Churches in 1950.

The grass roots reaction against socialism during the twenties did not prevent Marxian Socialists from creeping into strategic positions in the leadership of the Protestant Churches. The Marxian strategy was to get a few influential leaders to recite the Marxist line in the belief that many liberal ministers would eventually parrot what the key leaders said.

Consequently, the Marxists cultivated leaders like Lewis O. Hartman, editor of *Zion's Herald;* Harry F. Ward, founder of the Methodist Federation for Social Service; Jerome Davis, leading

light of the National Religion and Labor Foundation; and Sherwood Eddy, Kirby Page, and Reinhold Niebuhr, who were charter members of the
Fellowship for a Christian Social Order which
later became the Fellowship of Reconciliation;
also G. Bromley Oxnam who became a crusading bishop of the Methodist Church. These were
only a few of the Marxian Socialists in the
leadership of Protestant Churches, but they were
among the most influential.

There was a new tone of belligerence about
these men that was unknown to the social gospel-
lers. Ward, Davis, Page, Eddy, Niebuhr, and the
like had very little in common with the mystical,
pious Walter Rauschenbusch or the practical
Washington Gladden, although the Marxians traded
freely on the Gladden and Rauschenbusch names.
And they were justified in doing so for while
neither Ely, Gladden nor Rauschenbusch were
Marxians, Marxian socialism was the natural
offspring of the humanism of the Social Gospel.
Whittaker Chambers was right: Faith in Man
leads inevitably to communism.

Lewis O. Hartman, as editor of *Zion's Herald*,
filled that Methodist journal with good words for
Russian communism, such as ". . . ideals of
social justice and fair play, and the ultimate goal
of human brotherhood, the Marxian theory has
many similarities to Christian teachings" and
"Soviet Russia constitutes the greatest social
experiment in the history of the world. Never
before in the life of mankind has there been
an attempt on so vast a scale to equalize opportunity and to promote genuine brotherhood of
man."[23] The Methodists rewarded Hartman by
making him a Bishop.

Among the clerical apologists for Russia,
Harry F. Ward had the distinction of having his

membership in the Communist Party made public. Mr. Manning Johnson, a former leading member of the Communist Party in the United States, and Benjamin Gitlow, one time member of the executive committee of the Communist International and a member of its Presidium, and Mr. Louis Budenz, another notorious Communist leader who left the party all testified under oath before the House Committee on Un-American Activities that Harry F. Ward was a member of the Communist Party when they themselves were active in that Party.

Harry F. Ward

Harry F. Ward was born in England in 1873. He wanted to be a minister, but was too poor to get the necessary education. At the age of seventeen he migrated to Salt Lake City, Utah, worked at odd jobs for two years and later was able to study at the University of Southern California, finally receiving his A.B. from Northwestern in 1897 and his M.A. from Harvard in 1898. The following year he was ordained to the Methodist ministry and served churches in Chicago and Oak Park, Illinois from 1900 to 1912.

His left wing tendencies appeared early. In 1905, together with Oswald Garrison Villard and W. E. B. DuBois, he organized the Intercollegiate Socialist Society which helped establish the Rand School of Social Science in New York City. In 1907, he founded the Methodist Federation for Social Service of which he was the editorial secretary from 1907 to 1911 and general secretary from 1912 to 1945. According to Benjamin Gitlow, when the Communist Party was organized in the United States in 1919, the Methodist Federation for Social Service proved to be a useful tool. The Reverend Jack R. McMichael, one of

Ward's assistants in this organization, was a Communist Party member and leader of the Young Communist League.[24]

Although never an official organ of the Methodist Church, the Federation for Social Service could eventually boast of having in its membership seventeen Bishops and 4,000 clergymen and laymen. It spoke with authority and it spoke the Marxist line. It was not without criticism from within Methodism, but in defiance of all criticism it openly published its purpose in the October 1940 issue of *Social Questions Bulletin:* "The Methodist Federation for Social Service is an organization which rejects the method of struggle for profit as the economic base for society; which seeks to replace it with social-economic planning in order to develop a society without class distinction and privileges." Karl Marx could not have said it better.

Ward authored the Social Creed of the Church which he succeeded in getting the General Conference of the Methodist Episcopal Church to adopt in 1908. Immediately, the Federal Council of Churches adopted an almost identical statement. Other organizations echoed it. Twenty years later Harry F. Ward wrote in the *Christian Century* (April 19, 1928):

It is a revealing exercise to put in parallel columns the social creed of the churches; the earlier programs of organized labor, the Populists and the Socialists; the later platform of the progressive party, and the statement of social ideals adopted by members of the national conference of social work . . . When those who wrote the social creed, under the impulse of a long religious tradition, mentioned some of the things that the labor and farmer leaders and also the Socialists had been striving for, and when later the social workers and the progressives repeated in substance the main things that all the rest had said, it did not mean that any were borrowing language or ideas from others. It meant that a common movement in America life was coming to expression."

But all this similarity of ideas and language was not by chance! The "common movement in American life" that "was coming to expression" was the product of Harry F. Ward and his Marxian Socialist collaborators who were steering the many opinion forming organizations.

In 1913, Harry F. Ward went to Boston University, School of Theology, to be Professor of Social Service. Here a young student, G. Bromley Oxnam, made his acquaintance.

In 1918, the year Rauschenbusch and Gladden died, Dr. Harry F. Ward moved from Boston to New York to become Professor of Christian Ethics at Union Theological Seminary. Here he rendered valuable service — to the Communist Party.

Testifying under oath, Manning Johnson stated that Harry F. Ward had been "the chief architect for Communist infiltration and subversion in the religious field." [25]

Mr. Leonard Patterson, a former leader in the Communist Party, also told the same Committee: "While I was in Baltimore, two members who had graduated from Dr. Ward's Seminary came down to Baltimore for assignment to their ministerial duties; at the same time they came for assignment for their Communist duties from the section committee of the Baltimore section of the Communist Party. They were Party members when they got there. They explained that they were recruited as Party members by Dr. Ward while studying under him." [26]

During the twenties, the activities of the Marxian Socialists were confined largely to academic circles, labor unions, and the top level of the denominations. With the coming of the Great Depression of the thirties, they were able to capitalize upon that economic crisis to expand their reach.

"Capitalism is dead!" the Marxists shouted and Harry F. Ward shouted loudest of all. Writing in *The Christian Century* (February 3, 1932), he said:

> It is now widely recognized that the events of recent months mark the end of a period. Among the hard-headed this is simply an acceptance of the inevitable check to the financial prosperity that misled many into believing that we had discovered the secret of eternal youth for the capitalistic order. With the idealists who think in economic terms it is capitalism itself that is now passing. As a matter of fact what was finished is the era of expansion for capitalistic industrialism.

The seeds Ward and his helpers had sown in the twenties bore abundant fruit in the thirties. For example, in 1934, at Oberlin, Ohio, the Congregational Churches officially launched their Council for Social Action. Dr. Hubert C. Herring, Jr., a graduate of Union Theological Seminary, was chosen to be its first director. In the address he delivered on the occasion he said:

> It is revolution. The old patterns are torn up. Rugged individualism, the sacred right of capitalism, the vaunted right of a man to run his business as he sees fit without regard to the right of society, are dead . . . The profit motive rules supreme in the industrial era. The profit motive stands bankrupt, shivering and shaking as the chill winds of economic revolution bear down upon it. The day of the profit is done, in any such sense as the word has been used during the past one hundred years. The assumption by the state of the principle of responsibility for the welfare of all its citizens carries the corollary of increased taxation . . . 27

The General Council then climaxed its meeting by passing a resolution that could have come straight out of the *Communist Manifesto!* Following a series of "Whereases" which expounded a Marxian interpretation of the depression, tracing it to exploitation and class conflict, it asserted:

"Be it resolved that:

"We set ourselves to work toward:

"The abolition of the system responsible for these destructive elements in our common life, by eliminating the system's incentives and habits, the legal forms which sustain it, and the moral ideals which justify it."

When the delegates to this Oberlin Conference read this resolution in the next day's paper, most of them were shocked. The Marxists had waited until most of the delegates were on their way home before presenting this item of business. Consequently, less than one-fourth of the voting membership took action on it.[28] Nevertheless, we are indebted to these Marxists for giving us a clear revelation of their goals: the destruction of the capitalistic system, its incentives, habits, legal forms, and morals! There is nothing like knowing exactly what the preacher is trying to do!

How widespread was Marxian socialism among the rank and file of ministers? Kirby Page answered that question in 1934. He said: "Among all the trades, occupations, and professions in this country, few can produce as high a percentage of Socialists as can the ministry."[29]

Kirby Page should have known. He conducted a poll that year, mailing a questionnaire to 100,499 clergymen. Roughly 20% responded, or 20,970, which is a very poor response. Of that 20% only 5% preferred capitalism to a "cooperative commonwealth." Since a "cooperative commonwealth" was not defined, this reply means very little. When asked which political system would bring about this "cooperative commonwealth" about 56% answered "drastically reformed capitalism" and 28%, or 5,879 selected socialism.

The poll was not scientifically designed and consequently the results are not projectable.

However, from this poll it is at least apparent
that almost six thousand Protestant ministers
were willing to *go on record publicly* as favor-
ing socialism. From this one can conclude that,
while it would be a mistake to write off all Protestant   ministers   as   Socialists   during   the
thirties, socialism had penetrated the ministry
at the local level to a significant degree.

These were the days when Social Action became the fad. What was meant by this new phrase
in the ecclesiastical gobbledegook? Unlike the
Social Gospel which had a clearly defined body
of   doctrine   however   false,   Social   Action   has
been   vague   and   amorphous   in   its   theological
foundation. Only its goal has been crystal clear:
more government. Until recently, the intellectual
climate of Social Action has been Marxian, but
the best way to understand its rationale is to
examine the thought of its high priest, Reinhold
Niebuhr.

Reinhold Niebuhr

Reinhold Niebuhr was reared in the Evangelical
branch of the Evangelical and Reformed Church
in which his father was a pastor. Consequently,
he matured in an atmosphere saturated with Reformation thought and language. He studied at
Elmhurst   College   and   Eden   Theological   Seminary, but received no degree from either. When
he applied to enter Yale Divinity School, it was
without a college degree. Later, he humorously
explained that Yale Divinity School took him in
because they were short of students, but it is
more likely that they recognized a good student
in the young Niebuhr.

He   received   his   B.D.   from   Yale   Divinity
School in 1914 and his M.A. in 1915. Further
graduate study was made impossible by the death

of his father and he accepted a pastorate in Detroit where he remained from 1915 to 1928.

Articles began flowing from his pen as soon as he settled in the parsonage. The Ford Motor Company was a favorite whipping boy. "How Philanthropic is Henry Ford?" he wrote for *Christian Century*, December 9, 1926, making the absurd argument that, although Henry Ford paid the highest wages in the industry, he was still exploiting workers because of the long periods of idleness every year while plants were retooling for new models.

During this period he was much in demand as a speaker on college campuses, and together with Sherwood Eddy and Kirby Page, he was a leading light in the Fellowship for a Christian Social Order which in 1928 became the Fellowship of Reconciliation. These contacts paid off. His close friend, Sherwood Eddy, persuaded the faculty of Union Theological Seminary (which included Harry F. Ward) to call him to the Chair of Christian Ethics in 1928. If entering Yale Divinity School without a college degree was unusual, teaching in Union Theological Seminary without either a college degree or an earned doctorate was miraculous. This miracle was a testimony to Niebuhr's unusual brilliance, and to the persuasive power of his Marxist friends.

In 1931, he shared with Roswell O. Barnes, John C. Bennett and others the distinction of organizing the Fellowship of Socialist Christians whose statement of principles was critical of the pacificism and optimism of the Social Gospel:

The Fellowship of Socialist Christians is a group who are agreed in their conviction that a Christian ethic is most adequately expressed and effectively applied in our society in Socialist terms. They believe that the Christian Church should recognize the essential conflict between Christianity

and the ethics of capitalistic individualism. They believe
that the evolutionary optimism of current Liberal Christianity is unrealistic and that social change fundamental enough
to prevent destructive social upheaval will require a combination of social intelligence and ethical vigor not yet in
sight . . .

If this was a break with the nonviolence of the
Social Gospel, three years later Niebuhr was to
make an even more significant break. He was
among sixty members of the pacificist Fellowship of Reconciliation who withdrew from that
organization over the question of the use of
force. The sixty who withdrew accepted the
Marxian position that armed force should be
used in the class struggle! [30]

During the thirties, Niebuhr's frankly Marxian
books were rolling off the press greeted with
flowers and applause from the *New York Times*.
Typical of these was *Reflection on the End of An
Era* (1934) in which he predicted "the end of
capitalism will be bloody, rather than peaceful."
Marxism, he said, was "an essentially correct
theory and analysis of the economic realities of
modern society" (pp. 24 and 30). He contributed
"After Capitalism — What?" to *World Tomorrow*
(March 1, 1933) in which he stated that if anything
was clear in March 1933 it was "that capitalism
is dying . . . that it ought to die."

The New Deal did not move far enough toward
socialism to please him. Socializing the means
of production he believed to be "a primary
requisite of social health in a technical age."
He also opposed Roosevelt's foreign policy until
Munich. Then, he suddenly became a Roosevelt
supporter. Finally, no one worked harder to involve our country in World War II.

During the forties, he entered a second phase
of his career in which he completely abandoned

pacificism and joined with John C. Bennett and others to found *Christianity and Crisis* to urge a head-on attack against Nazi Germany.

In *Christianity and Power Politics* (1940) he demolished the pacificist argument. By now, Niebuhr was fascinated by power and he turned to a study of St. Augustine, Luther, and Calvin seeking answers. Out of this came *The Nature and Destiny of Man* (1934) in which he probed deeply into the problem of evil. This book was probably his greatest work in spite of the inaccuracies scholars find in it.

The following year, in *The Children of Light and the Children of Darkness,* Niebuhr raised the question: how can one socialize property without "creating pools of excessive power in the hands of those who manage both its economic and political processes?" His study of sin gave Niebuhr some healthy misgivings about Marxism.

In the 1950's, he entered his third phase in which he rejected Marxian socialism. In 1956, he wrote: "I am not...able to defend, or interested in defending any position I took in *An Interpretation of Christian Ethics.*"[31] *An Interpretation of Christian Ethics* was written in 1935 during his most virulent Marxian period. By 1956 — and probably earlier — Niebuhr was done with Marxian socialism as he had formerly turned against the pacificism and optimism of the Social Gospel. However, his rejection of Marxism did not mean that he rejected the trend toward big government and a welfare state in our economy, nor that all Protestant ministers followed in his train.

Other Marxian Activists

There were other Marxian Socialists whose influence should not be underestimated because they did not sweep the heavens like Reinhold Niebuhr's meteor. They were activists rather than theorists or brilliant writers.

One such activist was Bishop G. Bromley Oxnam — one time student and friend of Harry F. Ward. He was one of the loudest voices in American Protestantism calling for diplomatic recognition of Soviet Russia before our government recognized Russia in 1933.

The 1940's were his heyday, however. During these years, he threw his support behind the Communists in the Spanish Civil War. At the invitation of Professor Dirk J. Struik, Bishop Oxnam became a sponsor of the National Council of American-Soviet Friendship. As president of the Division of Foreign Missions of the Board of Missions and Church Extension of the Methodist Church, on May 29, 1947, he mailed to all Methodist ministers a copy of Jerome Davis' pro-Communist book, *Behind Soviet Power*. Of course, this was done at the expense of the Methodist missionary budget.

Oxnam was also editorial adviser of *The Protestant Digest*, a magazine declared to be subversive by the House Committee on Un-American Activities. In fact, he was associated with so many questionable organizations and activities that the House Committee on Un-American Activities finally called him to appear before them in July, 1953. After a tumultuous examination, the Committee exonerated the Bishop of membership in the Communist Party, but charged him with having used the prestige of his office to promote Communist causes. Bishop Oxnam admitted that some of the organizations he had sponsored had turned out to be Communist connected, but he explained that he was ignorant of such connections when he became associated with them.[32]

Can Bishop Oxnam's plea of ignorance be extended to his anti-capitalistic pronouncements? Did he not know what he was doing when he lauded Sidney and Beatrice Webb in *Personalities in Social Reform?* Concerning these two English Fabian socialists he said: "These devoted scholars are chiefly responsible for the social reform that marks the passing of Britain from a capitalist empire to a socialist commonwealth."

All Marxians in the Protestant ministry were not as influential as Bishop Oxnam, nor as forthright as Claude Williams. Williams admitted that the only reason he joined the ministry was to facilitate his preaching of communism. For his blunt confession, he was unfrocked by the Presbyterian Church, U.S.A. in 1954. In 1965, however, a Negro Baptist Church in Detroit returned him to the ministry. He was reordained in the Hartford Baptist Church of Detroit, May 1965. Asked about his plans for the future, the reordained minister said: "I'm going to preach about an unholy Trinity — Unemployment, Race Discrimination, and Poverty — and these are behind the Negro Revolution in this country..."[33]

Few were as honest as Norman Thomas who left the Presbyterian ministry to become the Socialist Party's candidate for president from 1926 until he decided that it was useless to run any more because the Democratic Party had taken over all the measures he had been fighting for. A convinced Socialist, Norman Thomas has always been an anti-Communist.

Dr. Willard E. Uphaus was executive secretary of the National Religion and Labor Foundation, an organization Robert Moats Miller in *American Protestantism and Social Issues* described as coming "periously close to representing the

Marx-Lenin position" (p. 93). However, Uphaus
went a little too far to the left for even this
Foundation. They removed him as executive
secretary in 1950 because of his participation in
the Communist Warsaw Peace Conference.

Nine years later, the Superior Court of New
Hampshire sent Dr. Uphaus to jail for contempt
of court. Willard Uphaus refused to reveal the
names of his guests at a World Fellowship summer camp in Conway, New Hampshire. The
Attorney General said that he had "reliable information" that some of Uphaus' guests were
Communists. In view of Uphaus' record, this is
not hard to believe.

Bishop Francis J. McConnell, president of the
Federal Council of Churches from 1928 to 1932,
assisted Jerome Davis and Willard Uphaus in
organizing the National Religion and Labor Foundation in 1932. McConnell had been Harry F.
Ward's expediter in the Methodist Federation
for Social Service. Here, as elsewhere, McConnell's contribution was in shrewd strategy and
tactics. McConnell got things done.

During the thirties and forties, Marxian socialism in America produced a mushroom growth
of such left-wing religious organizations — always advertising a high-sounding purpose. Curi-
ously, the same names seemed to bob up in the
leadership of many of these religio-political
structures. The plan seems to have been to reach
as many different segments of the Protestant
population as possible by means of overlapping
organizations engineered by the same few at the
top.

To turn from the activists to the academicians,
John C. Bennett, who had shared with Reinhold
Niebuhr in organizing the Fellowship of Socialist
Christians in 1931, was called to be Professor of

Social Ethics at Union Theological Seminary in 1943. There followed a spate of books from his pen expounding the usual Marxian point of view, but, like Niebuhr, he was to become disillusioned with Marxism — a disillusionment that marked the beginning of a new phase of the collectivist movement in American Protestantism.

III. Keynesian Socialism

In "The Extension of the State's Role in Economic Life" which appeared in *Social Action*, March 1963, John C. Bennett, former agitator for Marxist socialism, declared that three features of capitalism should be preserved; namely, the capitalistic characteristic of multiple centers of power and initiative; the profit motive; and a modified form of the market mechanism.

This is a far cry from what Bennett was writing in the 1940's. In this same article, he also confessed that he had learned much from collaborating with economists for some years past. Although Bennett's concessions to capitalism sound good, we should have a look at those economists from whom Bennett "learned much."

In 1949, the Federal Council of Churches initiated a study of Christian Ethics and Economic Life which was taken over by the National Council in 1950. Over ten volumes were planned. Professor Howard R. Bowen was economic consultant to the study, and helped formulate the project and criticize the manuscripts. He also authored one of the books, *Social Responsibilities of the Businessmen*. From 1952 to 1955, Professor Bowen was professor of economics at Williams College, the alma mater of John C. Bennett.

For the most part, the economists who wrote

chapters or books in this series were Keynesians
of varying degrees. Neo-classical economists
were conspicuous by their absence. It was from
such Keynesians that Bennett "learned much."

Who was John Maynard Keynes?

John Maynard Keynes was born in England in
1883, the year Karl Marx died. His father was an
economist before him so, like John Stuart Mill,
he was reared in the atmosphere of economic
theory. The young Keynes sailed through Eton
and Cambridge with ease and success. While at
Cambridge, he joined the Fabian Society. In 1913,
he became secretary of the Royal Economic Society and cooperated with Sidney Webb to make
that society a vehicle of Fabian socialism.

During World War I, he was a member of the
British Treasury and represented the Treasury
at the Versailles Peace Conference, castigating
the Treaty which he saw emerging from their
deliberations. In anguish, Keynes finally resigned
from the Treasury and wrote *The Economic
Consequences of the Peace,* a prophetic analysis
of the Versailles Treaty.

Keynes then went into finance; managed an
investment trust; guided the finances of a life
insurance company; wrote for the *Manchester
Guardian;* and taught at Cambridge. In his spare
time, he wrote a book on mathematics — *Treatise
on Probability.* By 1923, he got around to his
chief interest and published *Tract on Monetary
Reform* and in 1930, *Treatise on Money.*

By this time the depression was upon the
western nations and John Maynard Keynes became absorbed in the problem of the business
cycle. By 1936, his best known work, *General
Theory of Employment, Interest, and Money,* had
appeared.

Regarding this book, Keynes wrote George

Bernard Shaw, the notorious Fabian Socialist: "To understand my state of mind, you have to know that I believe myself to be writing a book on economic theory which will largely revolutionize — not, I suppose at once, but in the course of the next ten years — the way the world thinks about economic problems."[34]

His prediction about this has been as accurate as his prediction concerning the ill-fated Versailles Treaty. Keynes *General Theory* has been as revolutionary as Marx's *Das Kapital.*

As a result of *The General Theory*, John Maynard Keynes became — in the words of Wilhelm Roepke — "the intellectual authority for the economic policy in National Socialist Germany."[35]

Keynes was a mathematician and the system he developed — unlike crude Marxism — was a sophisticated, mathematical justification for a managed economy. Keynes called for an increased role of the State, explaining in *The General Theory:* "The State will have to exercise a guiding influence on the propensity to consume partly through its scheme of taxation, partly by fixing the rate of interest and partly, perhaps, in other ways" (p. 378). One of the "other ways" was the abandonment of the gold standard and deliberate inflation until the "functionless investor" was destroyed and the financiers and entrepreneurs were "harnessed to the service of the community." This Fabian had a special grudge against "rentiers," i.e. those who live on income from investments.

John Maynard Keynes said — in effect — you cannot depend upon the market to regulate the economy by supply and demand. Government must regulate it! He harped upon this point because the classical economists had assumed an orderly universe in which the market expresses the laws of nature. The classicists believed that men may discover these laws, but they cannot change them.

Keynes rejected all this. He argued that the market is not automatic. Man must master it, and he masters it by putting it under the control of Providential Government.

The Protestant leaders of Social Action persuasion agreed with Keynes. They had long since tossed out the doctrine of Divine Providence. Reinhold Niebuhr in an article, "The Providence of God," which appeared in *Advance*, June 14, 1954, declared: "It is not true... that there is a simple moral meaning to history and that the providence of God will inevitably assure the vindication of the 'moral law.'"

This is the watershed. If God cannot be counted upon for distributive justice, then men must turn to the State. And as men turn to the State to achieve distributive justice, they inevitably make a God of the State and become its servants.

Professor Alvin H. Hansen, formerly of Harvard, has been called "the American Keynes" because of his enthusiasm for Keynesian economics. In *Economics Issues of the 1960's* he spelled out what this kind of economics means for Americans in this last half of the century. In short, it means private ownership of the means of production. This, Hansen conceded, the Socialists of Europe have admitted is the only way to produce efficiently. But Keynesianism also means increasing government control and *socialization of the distribution.*

Hansen spoke of a "partnership" of private enterprise and government, but it is the partnership of a lion and a lamb in which the lion gobbles up the lamb! He said: "The role of government will increasingly be that of providing a wide range of services — those services which we have come to associate with the welfare state — social security, health, housing, education, recreation, and cultural programs and community projects" (p. 93). Whoever gains that much control over society will control the thoughts and souls of the people!

John Maynard Keynes has been represented as the saviour of capitalism, but what kind of capitalism will Keynesian economics save? A capitalism in which the rentiers are eliminated, not by armed revolution, but by the slow process of monetary management? A capitalism in which government furnishes most of the capital and closely controls the use of it? A capitalism in which government guides consumer spending by its tax structure? A better name for such a system would be Keynesian socialism, which is only a modern edition of Fabianism. It is much nearer the socialism of Nazi Germany, but more subtle, more efficient — and equally destructive of individual liberty.

By the 1950's, the better informed Social Action leaders knew that Marxian economics was a failure even in Russia where it has had ample opportunity to demonstrate its efficiency. Keynesian socialism furnished them with a new rationale for their collectivist, statist movement. Furthermore, unlike Marxism, it was respectable, having the support of a large wing of the economics profession in America. So they embraced it.

This does not mean that there are no longer any Marxists or Communists in the Protestant Churches. They are still at work. Moreover, other forces continue to threaten the free, individual tradition of Protestantism. Many Protestant leaders are doing their utmost to merge

as many Protestant denominations as possible to
increase the political power of the churches. The
National Council of Churches is slowly becoming
an arm of the government as it accepts and
administers Federal funds for a growing list of
welfare activities.

But the greatest danger of all to American
liberty both within and without the Protestant
Churches is from the Keynesian socialists who,
like their Fabian counterparts, avoid direct conflict with capitalism, and are accomplishing the
socialization of the economy so subtly that the
average citizen is unaware of what is happening.

Call the end result by any name you wish — a
managed economy, the Leviathan of Thomas
Hobbes, or the Beast State of Revelation 13 — it
is what Whittaker Chambers warned would come
to pass whenever men reject Faith in God and
substitute Faith in Man.

It is ironical that this substitution has been
most thorough-going in the House of God!

The God-is-dead theologians have startled a
great many laymen who had always assumed
that the reason for the Christian Church was
the existence of God. They would not have been
startled if they had kept up with the collectivist
movement in Protestantism. As we have discovered, that movement steadily shifted the center of Christianity from God to Man.

The late Paul Tillich taught the equivalent to
a God-is-dead theology in both Union Theological
Seminary and Harvard Divinity School for over
thirty years. In 1923, Reinhold Niebuhr, impressed by the socialism of this German theologian, helped bring him to Union where he taught
until 1955 when he moved to Harvard. In 1962,
he became professor of Theology at the University of Chicago. He died in 1965.

Paul Tillich was an existentialist in the tradition of Nietzsche who in the late nineteenth century announced to the world that God was dead. Dr. Tillich rejoiced with Nietzsche in the death of the God of theism and explained that God cannot be spoken of as "existing" or "not existing." For Tillich, the word "God" was but a symbol.

It is significant that, although he is reported to have rejected some Marxist views, Tillich was a convinced Socialist. Thus, this man for whom faith was not belief in God illustrates the basic difference between the civilization born of Christianity and the movement both within and without the Church which threatens its very existence. When you strip away all rationalizations, inconsistencies, and verbal razzle-dazzle, that difference can be summed up by one word: GOD!

Herman
Otten

Chapter 2

America's Moral Revolution

EROSION OF MORALITY

Herman Otten

Herman Otten is the pastor of Trinity Lutheran Church, New Haven, Missouri. He received his elementary education in the public schools of New York City and is a graduate of Concordia Collegiate Institute, Bronxville, New York. In 1957 he graduated with a B.D. from Concordia Seminary, St. Louis, and with an M.A. from Washington University. In 1958 he received his S.T.M. from Concordia Seminary.

Recognized as a spokesman for conservative Christianity, the author has lectured widely before groups of many denominations. He has debated with liberal clergymen and is the regular speaker on The Trinity Hour, a weekly radio broadcast.

The author is also the editor of *Lutheran News,* a bi-weekly newspaper with readers in all 50 states and some 40 foreign countries. The paper is "published in the interest of historic Christianity, Biblical missions, and true Christian unity." He recently wrote *Baal Or God.*

America's Moral Revolution

EROSION OF MORALITY

by Herman Otten

Morality is one of the most intensely discussed subjects in America today. *Look* said in an article on "America's Mood Today" that "Americans are living through a revolution in morality — particularly sexual morality."[1] Editors, law enforcement officials, college professors, politicians, clergymen, and many others have deplored the current lawlessness in the United States and the erosion of America's moral standards. The *San Francisco Examiner* stated in a widely circulated editorial on "The Appalling Erosions Of Moral Standards":

WHAT HAS happened to our national morals?

An educator speaks out in favor of free love.

A man of God condones sexual excursions by unmarried adults.

Movies sell sex as a commercial commodity.

Book stores and cigar stands peddle pornography.

A high court labels yesterday's smut as today's literature.

Record shops feature albums displaying nudes and near nudes.

Night club stage shows that would have shocked a smoker audience a generation ago.

TV shows and TV commercials pour out a flood of sick, sadistic and suggestive sex situations.

A campaign is launched to bring acceptance to homosexuality.

Radio broadcasts present discussions for and against prom-
iscuity.

Magazines and newspapers publish pictures and articles that
flagrantly violate the bounds of good taste.

Four letter words once heard only in barroom brawls now
appear in publications of general distribution.

Birth control counsel is urged for high school girls.

Look around you. These things are happening in your America. In the two decades since the end of World War II we
have seen our national standards of morality lowered again
and again.[2]

Jenkin Lloyd Jones, editor of the Tulsa, Oklahoma, *Tribune*, told the American Society of
Newspaper Editors at New Orleans that "the
Jeremiahs haven't been so wrong, after all. It is
sad to watch the beginnings of decay." Jones
said in his address, which has now been reprinted
in newspapers and magazines throughout the nation: "But the Age of Fakery in art is a mild
cross that American civilization bears. Much
more serious is our collapse of moral standards
and the blunting of our capacity for righteous
indignation."[3]

Former President Dwight D. Eisenhower deplored the breakdown of law and order on September 1, 1965 in a dedicatory address. He said:
"I'm concerned about a general disregard for the
moral law and the legal law in this country."[4]

The grim statistics of crime in the United
States from the Federal Bureau of Investigation's
annual report for 1964 showed that the nation's
crime rate went up 13 per cent over 1963. In
the six years since 1958, the number of crimes
of violence has gone up 40 per cent; crimes
against property, 61 per cent. In the same period,
U.S. population has risen 10 per cent.[5] *U.S. News
and World Report* said that "Violent crime is
now running wild in the cities and suburbs of the

United States.

"The crime rate since 1958 has shot up almost six times as fast as the rise in population. In 1964, there occurred a virtual explosion of crime."[6] The December 25, 26, 1965 *St. Louis Globe Democrat* reports FBI Director J. Edgar Hoover as stating: "The first six months of 1965 saw serious crime increase 5 per cent over the same period in 1964."

Evangelist Billy Graham wrote in 1965:

Jesus indicated that as men approached the end of history there would be worldwide rebellion against law and order. Rebellion and lawlessness are already present on a scale such as the world has never known. Children rebel against their parents until many parents are actually afraid of their children. Young people rebel against their teachers. University students rebel against administrative authorities. There is an organized attempt to downgrade the policeman, to make fun of him and despise him. All this is part of a general disrespect for law and order.[7]

David L. McKenna, president of Spring Arbor College and former director of The Center of Higher Education at Ohio State University, said: "We are in the throes of a Moral Revolution, defined by Robert Fitch as a 'Sexplosion.' We are reaping the results of an affluent permissive and sex-suffused society. The center of this revolutionary storm is the college campus, and its object is the college student."[8]

Pitirim A. Sorokin, professor of sociology at Harvard, wrote in his *The American Sex Revolution* that "Our civilization has become so preoccupied with sex that it now oozes from all the pores of American life."[9] Sorokin points to the parallel between sex habits of ancient Egypt, Greece and Rome during their decadence and the present sex revolution in America.

Christian Economics reported that the Mattachine Society of Washington, a society organ-

ized to protect the rights and liberties of homosexuals, sent a letter to many, probably all, U.S.
Congressmen declaring that one out of every
ten American citizens is a homosexual, "including roughly a quarter million each in the federal
Civil Service, the armed forces, and security
positions in private industry, and at least ten
per cent of your constituents." *Christian Economics* observed that "Homosexuality accompanies
a declining civilization. The Bible speaks very
plainly on this subject, including St. Paul's
statement in Romans 1:24: 'Wherefore God also
gave them up to uncleanness through the lusts
of their own hearts, to dishonor their own bodies
between themselves.' "[10] Testimony by security
officers before a House Appropriations subcommittee in 1965 revealed that the State Department
in 1964 uncovered 46 "security risks" among its
personnel — 32 of them homosexuals. All 46
resigned from their jobs.[11]

Another destructive factor in America's moral
revolution is the wide circulation of obscene and
pornographic material. FBI Director J. Edgar
Hoover wrote in the January 1960 *FBI Law Enforcement Bulletin:* "The morals of America are
beseiged today by an unprincipled force which
will spare no home or community in its quest
for illicit profit." Jeffrey St. John, executive
editor of *Report Magazine* and radio news com-
mentator on New York City's nightly "Window
on the World" program, wrote: "A $2-billion-a-
year racket is eroding the foundation of Western
civilization. Its name is pornography, and its
only goal is 'the fast buck,' with no thought
given to its products — ruined lives and the
debasement of our young people's morals."[12]
According to a hearing before the Subcommittee
on Postal Operations, J. Edgar Hoover declared

that poronography threatens to "pervert an entire generation."[13]

THE CAUSE OF THE EROSION

While various reasons have been listed as the cause of today's moral erosion, the basic cause of our nation's lawlessness and sexual anarchy is that far too many no longer believe and trust in the true God. Daniel Lyons, S.J., writes: "Since religion has become separated from God in the modern mind, so has morality. The world today considers itself quite independent of God. The result is relativism, subjectivism, and man-made morals." The widely read columnist observes: "The greatest problem in America today is that the whole idea of right and wrong is being lost. There are no absolute standards. Everything is 'situation ethics,' which means you can justify anything you really want to. It all starts with a lack of belief, and even among Catholics there is growing confusion over what we believe."[14]

Far too many are following the humanists of our day who have repudiated God and Biblical standards of right and wrong. Dr. Brock Chisholm, one of the most influential of these humanists, who, according to 1964 reprint of his *Prescription For Survival*, was President of the World Federation for Mental Health and Vice-President of the World Association of World Federalists, wrote:

I think there is no doubt that this idea of sin creates much havoc in our relationships with other cultures, and that we should begin to think far more clearly and more extensively than we have in the past about it. We must remember that it is only in some cultures that sin exists. For instance, the Eskimos didn't have this concept until quite recently. Now they have; they caught it from us.[15]

When he delivered the William Alanson White

Memorial Lectures in Washington, D. C. in 1946,
Chisholm said:

. . . For many generations we have bowed our necks to the
yoke of the conviction of sin. We have swallowed all manner
of poisonous certainties fed us by our parents, our Sunday
and day school teachers, our priests, and others with a
vested interest in controlling us . . .

The reinterpretation and eventual eradication of the concept
of right and wrong which has been the basis of child training,
the substitution of intelligent and rational thinking for faith
in the certainties of the old people, these are the belated
objectives of practically all effective psychotherapy? Would
they not be legitimate objectives of original education? . . .
With the other human sciences, psychiatry must now decide
what is to be the immediate future of the human race. No one
else can.[16]

An Associated Press release in the December
12, 1965 Philadelphia *Sunday Bulletin* reported:
"Group of psychiatrists today urged colleges not
to worry about student 'sexual activity practiced
with appropriate attention to the sensitivities of
other people.'

"The report on 'Sex and the College Student'
was prepared by a committee of the Group for
the Advancement of Psychiatry, a nationwide
organization.

"The committee reported after a three-year
study, based in part on material from college
psychiatrists and other college officials, that
'for some adolescents, experimentation may be
important, committment would be premature, and
something is to be gained from a transitory relationship.'"

Hugh Hefner, the high priest of the $50,000,000
Playboy empire who finds nothing wrong with
pre-marital intercourse provided it involves no
coercion or exploitation,[17] is quoted in a *National Observer* article on "Religion and the
Playboy 'Philosophy'": "Somewhere along the
line, it became apparent to me that the traditional

religious concepts of heaven and hell, rewards
and punishment, and the view of life on earth as
only a preparation for an afterlife are really in-
credible concepts."[18] *National Observer* says
that Hefner's "theology is humanist, for he em-
phasizes faith in man and not faith in God. I'm
not an atheist, he says. 'If you're going to pin
me down, I suppose an agnostic. Life here on
earth — the interrelationship of human beings-is
fantastic. The notion of a God, a power that
created it all, is so completely overwhelming . . .' " *National Observer*, on the basis of
an interview with the creator of Playboy "philosophy", reported: "Mr Hefner believes Jesus was
not divine — a conviction shared, notes one
theologian, by 'half of liberal Protestantism.'
But he agrees thoroughly with what he considers
'the essential concept of Christianity,' the brotherhood of man."[19]

Stacey Hebden Taylor, an English clergyman,
writes that "Because the humanist thinks that
God is dead or does not exist, he argues that
all kinds of behaviour are now permissible,
including sexual intercourse between men." In
an article on "The New Legality" Taylor says:
"Finally, the advocates of the new morality and
new legality believe that the established religion
of the state must now become scientific humanism
rather than Christianity. A common faith in
man's capacity to save himself by his own planning, reason and science must replace the older
faith in Jesus Christ as man's only means of
salvation".[20]

Historians and sociologists tell us that lawlessness and sexual anarchy are marks of de-
caying civilizations. Christians recognize that
such moral erosion is evidence that death is
already at work in a society because many mem-

bers of that society have forgotten God.

MODERN LIBERALISM AND GOD'S LAW

What do modern liberal protestant churches have to offer in the present dilemma? Are they part of the disease -- humanism — or do they accept God's Law as it is recorded in Holy Scripture as an unchanging and objective standard of morality? The following quotations and reports demonstrate that modern theological liberalism is part of the disease.

A news release from Ottawa, Canada, reported:

> A chaplain at Carleton University has suggested that premarital sexual relations are justifiable if they contribute to personal growth.
>
> Writing in the *Carleton,* student newspaper at Carleton University, Rev. Gerald W. Paul representing the Anglican, Presbyterian and United Churches on campus said recently, 'only if we are certain the sexual relationship will help more than harm our partner, in the long run as well as in the immediate encounter, are we justified in permarital sex'.[21]

Called to Responsible Freedom: The Meaning of Sex in the Christian Life, published for The United Christian Youth Movement by the National Council of Churches of Christ in the U.S.A., endorses the modern revolt against the standards of sex revealed in God's Law. Here are a few exerpts from this NCC pamphlet:

> The man who really loves God and his neighbor doesn't need any laws or rules to tell him what to do or not to do . . . The difficulty with Western Society's legitimate regulation of sex conduct is that it has been far too negative and far too monolithic. . . . Our culture declares that all sexual activity within marriage is proper, and good, while any such activity outside marriage is illicit, sinful and wrong. This is to ignore the personal dimension of life, to seek to force everyone under on massive legal umbrella. You and I know perfectly well that there are many marriages that are simply matters of convenience, that such sex as goes on within them is selfish, exploitative, and evil. We know further that there is sexual contact between unmarried couples that is motivated by love and which is pure and on occasions beautiful . . .

The NCC pamphlet continues:

In the personal, individual sense, then, what justifies and sanctifies sexuality is not the external marital status of the people before the law but rather what they feel toward each other in their hearts. Measured in such a way, holding hands can be very wrong indeed while intimate sex-play can be right and good.

The NCC advises youth:

You have got to make up your own mind, in the best light of your own conscience, what your own standards of conduct are going to be, and then do your best to live up to them...[22]

An article in *Campus Encounter,* which is published by the United Campus Christian Fellowship, the campus movement of the Christian Churches (Disciples of Christ), Evangelical United Brethren Church, United Church of Christ and the United Presbyterian Church in the U.S.A., actually advocates the practice of free love with the elimination of marriage vows. The article titled, "Love Without Fear — A Personal View of Being Physical," says:

We would be naked together; we could touch each other. We naked people would be free and there would be no mistaking that; yet, we would be so free that all forms of expression would be so possible for us in this new world where people do not hide themselves that for us there would be no compulsion to use all the forms. And so, faithfulness and freedom would not be mutually antagonistic, we would not qualify freedom by demanding responsibility. Faithfulness and responsibility would not be rules enforced by guilt and jealousy or fear but would be a description of the way free men and women live together.[23]

In this new relationship of freedom, advocated in the *Campus Encounter,* "No knots would have been tied; no solemn rules enacted." The public- ation for college church youth says:

May I make it clear that I think these people would be free sexually in ways that are perhaps startling to us. Love would characterize their relationships with other people, and this love would not be some airy spiritual-intellectual phantasy that has nothing to do with flesh and blood; it would be a love of bodies in all their different aspects as well as a love of sensitivity and aspiration. It would be bisexual in that there would not be the kind of fear that keeps two men from embracing and showing affection in this society . . . For reasons I hope are now clear these people would not need to own their wives or husbands or friends; . . .[24]

While expressing some criticism of Hugh Hefner's Playboy "philosophy," a few liberal Protestants have defended some of Hefner's views. Rev. Duane Mehl, a staff member on the Board of Parish Education of the Lutheran Church-Missouri Synod, writes in the January 1966 *Arena,* a youth publication of his church: "I do not think that Hefner wants to declare against religion. Rather he wants religion to join him in smiting his own collection of demons: Laws which restrict economic freedom, racial inequities which stifle a whole people, censors which dampen creative artists, collectivists who inhibit the uncommon man." Mehl writes in this same article on "The Playboy Vision" in *Arena:* "Premarital sex is an ironic misnomer. The act of sex is a marriage. It produces between two people a fusion and a fellowship symbolic of Christ's love for the world and His relationship to His church.

"FOR THAT REASON the church cannot panic when Hugh Hefner and Alfred Kinsey say that pre-marital sex is as common as a Sunday afternoon drive in the park. It may be. If so, many 'marriages' are taking place unawares; and the church has that to declare as strongly as possible." This entire article was reproduced in the January 10, 1966 *Lutheran News*.

Bishop John A. T. Robinson of the Church of England is one of the advocates of the "new morality" of the humanists, which rejects divine sanction for any specific law, rule, or regulation.

This Bishop writes:

For nothing can of itself always be labelled as 'wrong'. One cannot, for instance, start from the position 'sex rela- tions before marriage' or 'divorce' are wrong or sinful in themselves. They may be 99 cases or even 100 cases out of 100, but they are not intrinsically so, for the only intrinsic evil is lack of love. . . . But we are bound in the end to say with Professor Fletcher: 'If the emotional and spiritual welfare of both parents and children in a *particular* family can be served best by divorce, wrong and cheap-jack as divorce commonly is, then love requires it'.[25]

Chastity is the expression of charity-of caring, enough. And this is the criterion for every form of behaviour, inside marriage or out of it, in sexual ethics or in any other field. For *nothing else* makes a thing right or wrong.[26]

At this point Bishop Robinson in a footnote cites an article by H. A. Williams, "Theology and Self-Awareness," in *Soundings.*[27] Howard Carson Blake writes in *Christianity Today:*

The article by Williams that Robinson cites give a sample of what is meant by the 'new morality.' 'Sexual intercourse outside marriage,' he says, 'may be often perhaps almost always, an exploitation, unilateral or mutual. But there are cases where it need not be and is not.' He takes examples from two recent films. The first portrays how a nervous sailor acquires confidence in himself through the way a prostitute give herself to him. 'What is seen is an act of charity which proclaims the glory of God,' says Williams. 'He (the sailor) goes away a deeper, fuller person than when he came in. The second film shows how a man strongly attracted by small girls finds the courage to go to bed with an older women. He does it, and 'they sleep together, and has been made whole,' Williams concludes, adding: 'and where there is healing, there is Christ, whatever the Church may say about fornication. And the proper response is — Glory to God in the Highest' (pp. 81, 82).

It is little wonder that Mr. Williams (Dean of Trinity College) refused to accept the challenge of the Archbishop of Wales, in correspondence in the *Church Times,* to state categorically that fornication is wrong. He obviously believes that it is right sometimes.

Another member of the group who has repeatedly made the headlines on the 'new morality' is Douglas Rhymes, canon of Southwark Cathedral seat of the very diocese in which Robinson is a suffragen bishop. Rhymes preached a

sermon in the cathedral last March that attracted considerable notice. *Time* magazine (July 26, 1963) quotes him as
saying: 'Christ nowhere suggested that marriage was the
only place where sexual relationships could take place.' Also
in that sermon he declared: 'A great deal of the prejudice
against homosexuality is on the grounds that it is unnatural.
But for whom? Certainly not for the homosexual.'[28]

Having rejected the basic doctrines of historic
Christianity many liberal protestant clergymen
also reject an absolute standard of right and
wrong. *Time* reported:

The 20th century's sexual revolution directly challenges
Christianity's basic teachings against fornication and adultery. Some progressive church thinkers now advocate a 'new
morality' to take account of these facts of life. What they
propose is an ethic based on love rather than law, in which
the ultimate criterion for right and wrong is not divine command but the individual's subjective perception of what is
good for himself and his neighbor in each situation.

More than 900 clergymen and students gathered last week
at Harvard Divinity School to ponder the new morality and
its significance for the church. Inevitably the speakers
reached no definite conclusions, but they generally agreed
that in some respects the new morality is a healthy advance,
as a genuine effort to take literally St. Paul's teachings that
through Christ 'we are delivered from the law.'[29]

The Christian Century quotes Professor Joseph Fletcher of the Episcopal Theological School
in Cambridge as stating at the conference on the
"New Morality" at Harvard Divinity School: "We
cannot dogmatize."

Any sexual act (hetero-, homo-, auto-) engaged in, in or out
of marriage, will sometimes be bad, depending on the situation . . . sex for procreation or sex in marriage only is to
me only warmed over natural law. . . The new morality
would deny this and say rather that the right of any sexual
act is to be determined by responsible calculation in the
situation, not by pre-fabricated calculations. I find it increasingly difficult to think in terms of right and wrong,
black and white. One gets to truth by exploring cases.[30]

According to the *Christian Century:* "Dr.
Fletcher held fast to one principle: 'You must as
responsibly as possible seek the good of your

neighbor.' All other principles could be secondary: 'Subordinate them to the demands of love in the situation.'"[31]

H. Edward Rowe wrote in an article titled, "Obscene Plays in Religious' Garb" for *Christian Economics:*

Those who are counting on the churches to strengthen the moral fibre of our nation will find cause for disappointment in certain plays produced by people officially associated with some of our major religious bodies. The church musicale, *For Heaven's Sake*, and the songplay, *Black Nativity*, are two notable productions.

For Heaven's Sake was originally produced and directed by Robert E. Seaver, director of religious drama at Union Theological Seminary in New York. It was written by Helen Lenore Kromer especially for the North American Ecumenical Youth Assembly which purported to offer Christian guidance to two thousand youth gathered at the University of Michigan. John S. Wood, chairman of the National Council of Churches' Department of Youth Work, served as Organizing Secretary of the Michigan assembly. A. Wilson Creek, who holds a youth leadership post with the World Council of Churches, was chairman of the Drama Committee. It was in response to inquiries by Wood and Creek that the play was written by Miss Kromer.

The script of *For Heaven's Sake* is a fantastic conglomeration of immoral, un-christian and unpatriotic expressions. Christ is downgraded as 'a flop at 33.' Amid lengthy sections with off-color sex overtones couched in crude language and dance interludes, God is pictured at the roulette table and Uncle Sam is referred to as 'Uncle Sap.' One line has a young girl responding to an approach by soliloquizing, 'To go or not to go to bed, that is the question . . .'

Black Nativity is a two-act song-play in feverish folkbeat, with a all-Negro cast. As vocalists sing, two dancers act out the story of Mary and Joseph. Mary's labor pains are portrayed with ballet antics. According to a press release, 'The Broadcasting and Film Commission of the National Council cf Churches of Christ in the United States has advised its members that *Black Nativity* would be a highly meritorious production for churches and church groups.'

One wonders how church leaders and groups can justify such mockeries in the light of the purpose of the church as enunciated by the Savior in the Great Commission.[32]

Rev. Howard Moody has gone so far as to sug-

gest in *Christianity and Crisis,* which lists
Reinhold Niebuhr and John C. Bennett as chair-
men of its editorial board, that "Vulgar speech
and four letter words are not blasphemous or
immoral, and our shame and prudery over them
are basically class matters." Moody writes:

> For Christians the truly obscene ought not to be the slick-
> paper nudity, nor the vulgarities of dirty old or young literati,
> nor even 'weirdo' films showing transvestite orgies or male
> genitalia. What is obscene is that material, whether sexual
> or not, that has as its basic motivation and purpose the de-
> gradation, debasement, and dehumanizing of persons. The
> dirtiest word in the English language is . . . the word 'nigger'
> from the sneering lips of a Bull Connor. Obscenity ought to
> be much closer to the Biblical definition of blasphemy against
> God and man.[33]

Reporting a dance program which took place
at Moody's church, *Christianity Today* said:

> Modern man's preoccupation with sex seems now to be
> taking on ecclesiastical aspects.
> At Judson Memorial Church (American Baptist) in New
> York's Greenwich Village, a dance program last month in-
> cluded a number in which a man and woman, both nude,
> moved across the stage in a face-to-face embrace.
> The pastor of the church, the Rev. Howard Moody, in an
> article earlier this year in *Christianity and Crisis* called for
> a new definition of obscenity.[34]

Some modern religious leaders are on public
record as pleading for "understanding" rather
than "shock" in regard to the topless dress fad.
Douglas White, pastor of St. Mary's Church at
Mudford, England, said in a sermon to his congregation:

> I don't suppose we'll see any girls in these dresses at the
> moment, but they would be as welcome as anybody else at
> my services. I would not turn any woman away from church
> because she was wearing a topless dress. The human body is
> something good and wonderful just as all of God's gifts are —
> like the air and the sea. The attitude shared by some people
> make it appear almost as if parts of the human body are evil.
> Restrictive practices in clothing can hamper the fullness of
> life.[35]

Other instances could be cited to demonstrate that many modern liberal clergymen have departed from Christian standards of morality. The "new morality" of Bishop Robinson and some of the others we have quoted is not restricted to a few isolated clergymen. Some of these men have been defended by the National and World Council of Churches and they have not been disciplined by their denominations. Theodore O. Wedel, Canon Theologian of the Cathedral of St. John the Divine, New York, and President of the House of Deputies, Protestant Episcopal Church, USA, commenting on Bishop Robinson's book, *Honest to God,* said:

The Bishop of Woolwich is not committing a crime in revealing to a wider public what has been going on for a generation and longer in the world of advanced theological learning. He is attempting to prepare the laity of the churches for readjustments in some of their naive, adolescent, often outdated, and even idolatrous conceptions of the Christian faith.

It is the business of our theologians to reinterpret the faith to each age of cultural change. *Honest to God* is simply a bold and, some theologians may say, premature opening of a Pandora's box of theological novelties under debate among doctors of the schools behind the scenes.[36]

HOMOSEXUALS AND THE MODERN CLERGY

One of the most shocking developments in recent years has been the changing attitude of some modern clergymen towards homosexuals. The January 3, 1965 *San Francisco Sunday Chronicle* reported:

Ministers of four denominations accused the Police Department yesterday of "intimidation, broken promises and obvious hostility" in breaking up a private benefit for homosexuals at California Hall Friday night.

The ministers co-sponsored the event. They charged they, too, had been harrassed by police officials and questioned at length about their 'theological concepts.'

The ball was attended by nearly 600 homosexuals and

their friends, and a dozen ministers, to raise funds to promote 'a dialogue between the church and the homosexual.'
Tickets for the event were arranged through sponsoring organizations.

The January 3, 1965 *San Francisco Examiner*
added in its report of the benefit:

As for the other guests, many males were in eye-dazzling
evening gowns, and a policeman was heard to estimate that
'out of 100 women, half were the genuine article.'

Yesterday, the seven ministers called in reporters to explain the aims and purposes of the Council for Religion and
the Homosexual and to protest what they called "bad faith"
on the part of the police who parked their patrol cars at
the ballroom entrance and photographed the guests as they
arrived.

The Rt. Reverend James A. Pike, Episcopal
Bishop of California, was reported by the *San
Jose Mercury*, January 19, 1965, as saying before
a Stanford law students forum: "It's time for
California to adopt 'humane' laws governing
abortion and homosexuality... Homosexual acts
between adults in private should not constitute a
criminal offense." Canon Robert W. Cromey, who
served for three years as Bishop Pike's assistant
and who together with some 30 other clergymen
formed the Council on Religion and the Homosexual, said that some homosexuals are church
members but many of them are alienated because
of the traditional moral attitude of the church
that homosexuality is sinful. Concerning the law
against homosexuality, Cromey is quoted in the
December 7, 1964 *San Francisco Chronicle:*
"Laws like this are just silly. Certainly, after
people are over 21, they should be able to have
sexual relations with a lamp, if they want to."

CIVIL DISOBEDIENCE
AND THE MODERN CLERGY

Lawlessness has undoubtedly been encouraged

in our nation because some churches and religious leaders have gone on record as recom-
mending civil disobedience. The Lutheran Church
in America at its biennial convention in 1964
voted to write into Church law the following
declaration:

"If and when the means of legal recourse have been exhausted or are demonstrably inadequate, Christians may then
choose to serve the cause of racial justice by disobeying a
law that clearly involves a violation of their obligations as
Christians. . ."[37]

Episcopalian laymen prevented their clerical
leaders from adopting a similar resolution on
civil disobedience, although the resolution had
the support of the House of Bishops of the Episcopal Church.[38] Martin Luther King has repeatedly said that "bad laws" are immoral laws,
and therefore are not really laws at all.[39] Various clergymen have followed Dr. King's defiance
of the law. Father Geno Baroni, who was one of
forty Roman Catholic priests who joined Protestant and Jewish clergy in the March 9, 1965
protest march in Selma, Alabama, led by Dr.
King, wrote: "I suppose some people were sur-
prised at the spectacle of priests and ministers
and rabbis — there were perhaps 300 or 400 of
us in that body of 2,000 marchers — coming out
to demonstrate in defiance of a Federal court's
injunction"[40]

While national leaders have been understandably cautious in criticizing clergymen for encouraging disobedience, the press reported on
August 25, 1965:

Senator Robert Byrd (Dem.), West Virginia, denounced
Monday as 'shocking' the conduct of clergymen who have
encouraged the violence in many parts of the nation, including Chicago, and Los Angeles.
'I desire to ask, as do other concerned Americans,' Senator Byrd said in a Senate speech, 'whether the actions in

Los Angeles, in Chicago and in Springfield, Mass., may be
said to be a logical outgrowth, in part, of the leadership of
certain clergymen who have stated that it is appropriate, and
even desirable, to disobey what they arbitrarily consider to
be 'bad' laws and to obey only laws which they label as 'good'
— in other words that it is morally right to resort to disobedience whenever a citizens's 'conscience' tells him that
a law is unjust . . .

'All too often, certain clergymen have overlooked opportunities to help and succor the multitude in their own neigh-
borhoods to participate in highly publicized 'non-violent'
activities elsewhere that have culminated, not unexpectedly,
in violence.'[41]

Retired Supreme Court Justice Charles Whittaker said in a speech on lawlessness before a meeting of the Tennessee Bar Association on June 17, 1965:

While I do not claim that all of our crime is due to any one
cause, it seems rather clear that a large part of the current
rash and rapid spread of lawlessness in our land has been,
at least, fostered and inflamed by the preachments of self-
appointed leaders of minority groups to "obey the good laws,
but to violate the bad ones" — which, of course, simply advocates violation of the laws they do not like, or, in other
words, the taking of the law into their own hands.

And this is precisely what their followers have done and
are doing — all under the banner of 'peaceable civil disobedience,' which they have claimed to be protected by the
peaceable-assembly-and-petition provisions of the First
Amendment to the United States Constitution.

Although such preachments and practices have become far
more vocal and widespread in our recent racial strife, they
did not have their origin in that strife, but, rather, in the labor strife, sit-ins and lie-downs of an earlier era.

More recently, certain self-appointed racial leaders,
doubtless recalling the appeasements and, hence, successes
of that earlier conduct, have simply adopted and used those
techniques in fomenting and waging their lawless campaigns
which they have called 'demonstrations.'

They have recently used these techniques to incite their
followers to assemble, from far and wide — often, unfortunately, with the encouragement and at the expense of well-
meaning but misguided church organizations into large and
loosely assembled groups, which may have regarded as
mobs, to wage what they have called "demonstrations" to

force the grant of 'rights' in defiance of the law, the courts and all constituted authority.[42]

HISTORIC CHRISTIANITY AND GOD'S LAW

Since modern theological liberalism has rejected the Holy Scriptures as God's divinely revealed inerrant Word, it really has no unchanging standard of morality. Historic Christianity, on the other hand, accepts the Holy Scriptures as God's revealed Word and considers God's Law recorded in the Bible as an absolute standard.

Jesus declared: "If ye love me, keep my commandments."[43] "He that hath my commandments, and keepeth them, he it is that loveth me."[44] God's Law is simply and clearly stated in the 10 Commandments. Here a Christian has an unchanging standard. These commandments are not the vain babblings of some unknown editor as some liberals contend, but they are the directly revealed word of the Almighty God Himself. Christ said: "Think not that I am come to destroy the law, or the prophets: I am not come to destroy, but to fulfill. For verily I say unto you, Till heaven and earth pass, one jot or one tittle shall in no wise pass from the law, till all be fulfilled. Whosoever therefore shall break one of these least commandments, and shall teach men so, he shall be called the least in the kingdom of heaven: but whosoever shall do and teach them, the same shall be called great in the kingdom of heaven.[45]

Both the Old and the New Testaments repeatedly condemn adultery. The Apostle Paul writes:

"Now the body is not for fornication, but for the Lord; and the Lord for the body . . . Know ye not that your bodies are the members of Christ? Shall I then take the members of Christ, and make them the members of a harlot? God forbid . . . Flee fornication. Every sin that a man doeth is without the body; but he that committeth fornication sinneth against his own body."[46]

According to God's Word, homosexuality is a sin and is to be treated as such. Paul wrote that when men turn away from worshipping the true God the crassest immorality, including homosexuality, will prevail.[47] The Bible also teaches that Christians are to obey the laws of the government as long as the government does not command the Christian to sin.

"Everyone should obey the government that is over him, because there is no government except that which is put there by God. God has ordered our government to be over us. Then anyone who is against the government opposes what God has ordered, and those who oppose will be condemned."[48]

While historic Christianity teaches that salvation is completely God's free gift and that no man can perfectly obey God's law, it has always recognized God's Law as an objective standard of morality. Christianity does not teach that it is up to each individual to decide what is right and wrong according to some vaguely defined law of love. As long as modern Protestant churches refuse to confess historic Christianity and accept the Bible as God's Word, they will only continue to contribute to the appalling moral erosion of our day. Churches which preach the Christ of Holy Scripture, who is both true God and true man, have the only real solution to the erosion of morals.

Edmund A.
Opitz

Chapter 3

CHURCHES IN POLITICS

EDMUND A. OPITZ

Edmund A. Opitz is a senior staff member of the Foundation for Economic Education and book review editor of *The Freeman*. He is an ordained minister, a board member of the Congregational Foundation for Theological Studies, and coordinator of the activities of The Remnant. This is a nationwide fellowship of ministers, predominately conservative or libertarian in their political and economic outlook. Mr. Opitz is a founder, and serves as the Hon. Secretary of The Nockian Society, an informal group of people interested in the work of Albert Jay Nock, American essayist and editor of the original *Freeman*.

Mr. Opitz took his college major in political science, with a minor in economics. He went on to get a theological degree, was ordained in the First Parish in Beverly, Massachusetts, and spent nine years serving three parishes in two states. During one pastorate he taught at Harrisburg Academy in Pennsylvania; during another, he was an instructor in government at Curry College in Boston. In World War II he served in India as a Red Cross Field Director.

He is the author of a book, *The Powers That Be*, dealing with the application of religious principles to economic and political problems, and the co-author of another on similar themes, *The Kingdom Without God*. He has written the Introduction to two other books and several short studies such as "Problems of Church and Society," and "Perspective on the Natural Law." His numerous articles and reviews have appeared in various publications: *The Freeman, Faith and Freedom, Christianity Today, National Review, The Contemporary Review, Modern Age, The Crozer Quarterly, Vital Speeches*, and others.

CHURCHES IN POLITICS

by Edmund A. Opitz

The contemporary religious scene exhibits several interesting facets, but its curious political bent strikes the observer as perhaps the most obtrusive. This chapter deals with several phases of the effort by the denominational and interdenominational hierarchies and bureaucracies — official Christianity — to mold the American churches into a politically potent ecclesiastical pressure group.

What are some of the symptoms of this power bloc in action? Politics, in our day, has taken to the streets, and anyone who scans the newspapers or views television must have noticed the sprinkling of clerical collars and religious habits among those engaged in protest marches, sit-ins, kneel-ins, and other demonstrations. Most of this clerical action is sponsored and financed by ideologically motivated national church organizations; but some, no doubt, is spontaneous. Let it be acknowledged at once that those who seek to obey God rather than man may sometimes find themselves in conflict with the rules men lay down. Fear of the Lord does not always coincide with mere law-abidingness. But, on the other hand, neither does it necessarily imply civil disobedience! No man and no organization has an infallible hot line plugged into the will of the Almighty giving instruction for particular cases,

and the overwhelming burden of proof is always
with those who refuse to abide by the orderly
processes of social intercourse — so long as
these avenues remain open to them, and as fluid
as they are at present. Performing public
charades in order to convey a message to legislators is a poor substitute for rational forms
of political discourse; it is a deteriorated form
of communication. What is responsible for the
posture these events have assumed? This is the
important question; not, Who's to blame for them?
Understanding will be best served if we probe
the background of men, ideas, and events during
recent decades, whose net impact has resulted
in today's critical situation, with churchmen and
others taking to the streets.

Another manifestation of direct ecclesiastical
political action occurred during the 1964 presidential election campaign. The church power
bloc made itself virtually an arm of the Democratic Party. Lacking the authority to excom-
municate those who might consider voting for the
Republican candidate, its spokesmen merely declared that no Christian could possibly vote for
Mr. Goldwater! When church leaders deliver
themselves in these terms to the people of a
nation which is at least vestigially Christian, an
incalculable blow is delivered to the chances of
the candidate thus victimized. The event is too
recent in memory to need documentation, but
here, for instance, is John C. Bennett, president
of the wealthiest and most prestigious of the
country's theological seminaries, writing in the
October 5, 1964, issue of *Christianity and Crisis*.
In popular parlance, this is a liberal or left-
wing journal. It was founded nearly twenty-five
years ago, mainly by John Bennett and Reinhold
Niebuhr as a vehicle for expounding the Christian

case for American entry into World War II. During the first quarter century of this journal, writes Dr. Bennett, "we have never allied ourselves with any political party." But neither have they ruled out the possibility "that occasions might arise when men and issues would become so identified that 'A Christian Journal of Opinion' might have to take sides on candidates for public office. This is such an occasion."

"We have no desire," Dr. Bennett continues, "to argue that Mr. Goldwater is an evil man. . . We point simply to the objective, unarguable conflict between his record and the judgments of the Christian churches on most of the major issues of social ethics in our time. We have in mind neither some imaginary consensus of church members nor the stands of the agencies specifically organized for social action. We mean the sizeable body of ethical convictions that have been endorsed, after long process of study and debate, by the major American denominations, by the National Council of Churches and by the World Council of Churches."

The major aim of this chapter will be to explore what Dr. Bennett refers to as "the sizeable body of ethical convictions. . ." The term "ethical" in this connection is somewhat misleading; it does not refer to such matters as personal integrity and probity. The "ethical convictions" under scrutiny are really a bundle of dubious economic and political nostrums whose proper generic name is Collectivism. This doctrine has several local labels, liberalism being the commonly accepted label here for the ideology which has sparked the New Deal-Great Society trend. Liberalism is the belief, in Reinhold Niebuhr's words, "that it is within the power and competence of the state to direct the political

and economic life of a technical society for the
purpose of assuring the general welfare. . ."
This sounds plausible to the uninitiated, until he
realizes what the state direction and control of
political and economic life means in practice.
It means that government — society's enforcement agency — regulates people in their occupations and other activities, thus making a command performance out of everyday affairs. Evil
as this is for the victims, it nevertheless sounds
good to the initiated because it is *their* program
which is being fastened on the nation by a powerful caretaker government, properly instructed as
to its duties by collectivist churchmen! This is
"social ethics" and "social engineering," and a
hint of what this program is may be gleaned
from the fourth count in Dr. Bennett's early
indictment of Mr. Barry Goldwater. "The Senator from Arizona is committed to a social and
economic individualism that was always falla-
cious and that has become peculiarly inept in our
age. He has opposed most of the legislation that
has helped improve health, education, housing,
relief of poverty, opportunity for the oppressed."
Dr. Bennett writes as if the above listed goods
result, not from production, but from legislative
fiat! As if there were some magic in the mere
passage of laws which, opening the doors of opportunity, would automatically make everyone
healthier, wealthier, and better educated!

There is an old line labor union slogan which
runs: "Agitate, Educate, Legislate," The ecclesiastical power bloc operates in all three areas.
It agitates in public places, and sometimes, un-
invited, on private property. It seeks to educate
and propagandize in a steady stream of books,
papers, journals and pamphlets — mostly paid
for by church people who do not share the senti-

ments broadcast in this material. And it works
directly on legislators. There is now a Religion
Row on Capitol Hill, with all the major denominations officially represented. The Washington
Office of the National Council of Churches is
there; so is the Baptist Joint Committee on
Public Affairs, the Department of Social Responsibility of the Unitarian Universalist Association,
the Friend's Committee on National Legislation,
the United Presbyterian Office of Church and
Society, the United Church of Christ Council for
Christian Social Action, the Methodist Board of
Christian Social Concerns, and others. The
stress in church lobbying is heavily on the
"moral," a politically astute tactic. For, as one
clerical lobbyist put it, "You can always fight
'politics,' but it's difficult as hell to fight 'morality.'" Thus does one member of a small army
of ecclesiastical lobbyists conceive his role: as
the voice of the "moral consensus" of the nation.
Those who are opposed to the economic and political program for which ecclesiastical officialdom
is lobbying thus find themselves shoved into an
awkward position — opposing the "moral consensus." They are not merely in error, they are
also in sin!

Most Americans cherish the principle of the
separation of Church and State. This doctrine is
an essential element of our Puritan heritage, it
is sanctified by long custom among us. The intent
of this principle, properly understood, is that the
purity of the Gospel shall be maintained. This
nation has never had an official religion, for good
and sufficient reasons. A number of the Colonies
and, later, several of the states did make tax
money available for denominational support. But
no religion has ever been established in the
United States; Church and State have each main-

tained an independent existence. The doctrine of
separation is an equation with two sides. On the
one hand, it is the conviction that the State must
not interfere with matters that are properly
within the domain of religion or the rightful
concern of religion. Balancing out this idea, is
the conviction that the Church, in the sense of
an official corporate body, shall not interfere in
affairs that are properly political. The Gospel
must not be politicalized; but neither must politics be gospelized. The principle of separation
is destroyed the moment either side violates it,
and both sides are guilty of violations today. The
equation tilts precariously.

When the proper sovereignty of each of these
two spheres — Church and State — is not maintained we have the condition often called "clericalism." Clericalism is almost universally
deplored; no American churchman defends it.
Here is how one of them describes it: "Clericalism is the pursuit of power, especially political power, by a religious hierarchy, carried
on by secular methods and for the purpose of
social domination. . .

"The goal of clericalism is to exert a decisive
influence upon the representative spheres of public life in the interests of the Church's secular
power. Clericalism seeks to shape the policies
of state, the composition of governmental departments, the expression of opinion, the ap-
propriation of funds, the forms of entertainment.
The process of achieving this goal involves the
use of pressures which are linked to subtle
forms of intimidation where resistance is
offered." *(U. S. News & World Report,* July 4,
1960)

Now, this sounds like a stinging rebuke to the
"agitate, educate, legislate" activities of church-

men described above. And it is, although such is
not the intention. This definition of clericalism
is from the pen of John A. Mackay, former president of Princeton Theological Seminary, and a
prominent political actionist churchman! Dr.
Mackay's rebuke is directed against what he
feels are the machinations of the Roman Catholic Church in various Latin countries, but any
unprejudiced observer would be compelled to
admit that his strictures are equally relevant
to the political activities of official church bodies
in this country, where Dr. Mackay himself is a
leading figure!

Clericalism is based on a faulty diagnosis of
the ills of society, and consequently it prescribes
the wrong remedy. Its sovereign remedy is collectivism; or, as it is usually termed, liberalism
— the good society by legislative fiat. Although
the leading ecclesiastical spokesmen for liberalism utter their present pronouncements with a
"Thus saith the Lord" finality, a probe into
their past reveals that these men have cham-
pioned contradictory courses with the same partisan zeal they now display on behalf of the Great
Society Program. The ordinary citizen arrives
at his convictions by reason, logic and intuition,
procedures which are open to all. He knows that
the Truth has not been delivered to him from on
high, and thus he maintains a sense of his own
fallibility. "To realize the relative validity of
one's convictions and yet stand for them un-
flinchingly is what distinguishes a civilized man
from a barbarian," wrote the noted economist,
Joseph Schumpeter.

The reluctance of the ecclesiastical social
action people to put themselves on an equal
footing with other men who are trying to mel-
iorate the problems of contemporary man and

improve society according to Christian norms, is
difficult to understand unless one realizes two
things. First, they believe — as they themselves
point out — that they are called upon to "witness
to the convictions of an advanced minority." In
order to do this, they need "prophetic freedom,
without being chained to any majority or consensus." They are fortunately placed, being lifted
above "the narrow class interests which unhappily
characterize large segments of their denominations." Thus they have "a broader perspective
than the average layman can hope to have."
Suburban churches are the butt of their scorn;
these are "bourgeoise ghettos." Secondly, these
people think in cloak-and-rubber-dagger terms
of infiltrating and capturing centers of power.
Christian Action was organized, mainly by
Niebuhr and Bennett, to "formulate strategies
for concerted effort in influencing power centers"
in church and society. "All of us are in position,"
declared its executive secretary to the membership, "and all of us can get ourselves into a
better position, to advance our common convictions through the religious institutions to which
we have direct access." Christian Action was
dissolved in 1956, its mission accomplished. Its
president announced that the appropriate departments of the National Council of Churches were
carrying out the task that Christian Action was
founded to accomplish, and thus there was no
need for a separate organization.

A major tactic employed by the social actionists to better their position is to impugn the
motives of all who are outside their camp. This
takes two forms, one general, the other particular. In general, every opponent of collectivism
or liberalism is charged with venality; the champion of the free market, private property, limited

government philosophy is said to have his eye on
the main chance, anticipating — as a writer in
The Christian Century puts it — "that a few rich
Americans can liberally endow propaganda in
favor of laissez-faire ideas. . ." In particular,
all church men who oppose the ecclesiastical
power bloc are accused of a kind of pietism
which would keep religion out of the everyday
affairs of life, away from the marketplace and
forum. Bishop James A. Pike, ecumenicist and
social actionist, has, in the course of his life
thus far, gone through two sets of major religious
beliefs and is now in his third. Nevertheless, he
is so certain of his present opinions that the
accuses all churchmen who do not share them of
wanting to retain their churches merely as private clubs where the members can huddle in
cozy spiritual warmth and polish ecclesiastical
brass. The then current president of the National
Council of Churches echoed these sentiments in
his inaugural speech. In years of combing social
actionist literature I have never encountered the
admission that there is a tenable position on
economic and political matters other than the
nostrum being peddled at the moment by the
social actionists! This is an unhealthy situation.

The corporate church, agitating, propagandiz-
ing, lobbying in support of a detailed program
of social reform is one way for the church to
"get into politics." It is not the only way, even
though it may be the only way recognized by the
ecclesiastical power bloc. That there is another
and better way has been pointed out by Dr. Walter
Judd, famed missionary and churchman, and
former Congressman from Minnesota. Address-
ing the delegates to the recent 11th Annual Meeting of the National Association of Congregational
Christian Churches in Pomona, California, Dr.

Judd said, "I don't want the church working in politics. I don't want political action by ecclesiastical bodies. I do want political action by Christians. It isn't the job of the church to say what you should do. It is the job of the church to change men and women and send them into society as Christian missionaries and into politics to help change the government."

We human beings, men and women, are here in the body, presumably, because this is a divinely ordained and indispensable means for finding out who we really are and what we may become. We are also in society, being made in part for mutuality and communion with our fellows, and we are laid under obligation to achieve in our social relationships such justice as is possible in the human situation. The built-in shortcomings of human justice, even at its best, convince the Christian, at least, that justice needs to be tempered and completed by love. But we also participate in another order of reality, St. Paul's "things that are not seen." The structures of politics do not endure, civilizations and cultures come and go; but if the Christian hope is to be trusted, the person is forever. Men are destined for ends which transcend the social order, but the integrities of the political and economic spheres of our lives must, on their own level, be respected. They are means, and if viewed in proper perspective, they are indispensible means for the realization of man's spiritual end as an immortal soul. The ultimate end is citizenship in The Kingdom of God, and this is not a state to be attained within history by human striving; it transcends the human and natural orders, being another dimension of existence.

St. Augustine's great fifth century work is *The City of God*. In it he wrote: "Two cities, for the present mingled together in body, but in heart, separated. One, whose end is eternal peace, is called Jerusalem, the other, whose joy is temporal peace, is called Babylon." Two orders interpenetrate, and man is a creature of both realms. If individual life is to be fruitful neither realm must be neglected, but the proper priorities must be established. When men neglect to seek first the Kingdom and try instead to make the social order autonomous, they fail even to maintain society in health. Lacking transcendent norms, the economic and political orders become ends in themselves, and men strive vainly to set up a kingdom of heaven on earth. Inevitably — if the ingredients of high religion are denied or neglected — some men will make an idolatrous religion of politics; and it takes but a numerically small group of fanatically dedicated men, forming a sect of political visionaries — the Communists, in our day — to swing the world off its proper axis.

The church is *in* the world, bearing witness to the fact that man is not wholly *of* the world. But the church is *of* the world, too, and in every age some churchmen have sought accommodation to the secular power. Often, even most of the time perhaps, the secular authority was wooed in the expectation that the two powers in conjunction would bring about better results than the church alone, limited to moral suasion and example, could hope to attain. From the time of Constantine down to the present day, the partnership of sacred and secular has again and again dashed the hopes pinned to it. Efforts by churchmen to convert the power of the state to serve sacred ends has resulted in the church being subverted to serve secular ends! The hand that wields the sceptre has proved ill-adapted to the sword, and vice versa. The history of the efforts to mix functions provides some of the most melancholy chapters in the saga of Christendom.

But as with the gambler, so with some churchmen in each generation. The lessons that should disillusion, generate instead a false hope that this time, working now with "democratic controls on power," will result in a success of such dimensions that the sting of past failures will be wiped out completely. For the first time in history, governments have been able to trick a lot of people into believing that popular welfare is now the goal of politics. It was difficult enough to keep Church and State separate when the latter projected the image of a warlord or policeman; but now that the State comes in the guise of a guardian angel some churchmen are more than ever tempted to politicalize their faith and get on the side of that angel! These men are doubly wrong. They are, in the first place, mistaken in their assumption that political action is merely another variety of group or cooperative action. Not so! Government is *the* power structure of a society, exercising the only power of its kind. To speak of other power structures in society is to employ a metaphor — unless, as frequently happens, government has deputized a private center with a share of its own power. Actually, every government, whatever its outward form — monarchical or democratic — operates with overtones of either overt or covert violence. Government is society's legal agency of coercion, and coercion is what it is, whether it be exercised by a king, a majority, a minority or whatever. Secondly, these men tend to forget that political action, whether benign or not, is no substitute for religious action. Religion has its unique functions to perform, and giving itself

over to the underwriting and sanctioning of any
political program or platform is not one of them.
Moreover, every liberal or collectivist program,
including that which has ecclesiastical endorsement, promotes the material well-being of some
men at the expense of others. Injustice is a built-
in feature of every form of collectivism — including Dr. Bennett's "sizeable body of ethical
convictions." A church which adapts itself to the
prevailing political fashions of the age runs the
risk of being discarded when the political style
changes — as change it will.

Thus, the broad picture. Influential churchmen
and theologians, operating through official church
agencies and organizations, have strained to the
task of molding the Protestant churches into a
politically potent Great Church for the Great
Society. Their joint efforts have not been for the
attainment of Christian unity for its own sake;
it has been unity-for-the-sake-of-power. The end
for which this power is to be used is something
called "social justice." More concretely, in the
words of the late Bishop B. Bromley Oxnam, in
1958, the aim is to create "a society fit to be
called the kingdom of God." It means, Niebuhr
told us in 1963, "the welfare state, the politics
of the New Deal. . ." It means a command soci-
eity, organized and operated bureaucratically,
employing, he declared, "all the instruments and
authority of the political state." This is despotism, of course, but the ecclesiastical liberals
tell us that it is not despotism per se that we
need fear; despotism in enlightened hands and
under democratic auspices to advance desired
national goals is not to be feared but welcomed.

This clerical program does not have a notice-
ably Christian ring to it, and indeed it does
little but add a bit of spiritual unction to the

contemporary program of secular liberalism, as exemplified by such an organization as Americans for Democratic Action. It may be noted also that contemporary "liberalism" does not have much about it that is Liberal, in the sense of Classical Liberalism!

Classical Liberalism proceeded in the tradition of old-fashioned Whiggism. The Whig Party contained errors, but it stood for freedom, and by freedom it meant a condition in society in which no man is subject to another man's will — "freedom under law." In practice, this meant customary, procedural, and constitutional restrictions on government — "limited government." Woodrow Wilson reminded us of this in his Cooper Union speech in New York in 1912, when he declared that: "The history of liberty is the history of the limitations placed upon governmental power."

Christianity, when true to its genius, also stands for freedom. De Tocqueville noted this in the 1830's. "In France," he wrote, "I had almost always seen the spirit of religion and the spirit of freedom marching in opposite directions. But in America I found they were intimately united and that they reigned in common over the same country." Edmund Burke, in the previous century, had spoken to Parliament of the Colonists' sense of personal independence, and the rootage of this individualism in their religion. "Religion, always a principle of energy, in this new people is not way worn out or impaired; and their mode of professing it is also one main cause of this free spirit. The people are Protestants, and of that kind which is most adverse to all implicit submission of mind and opinion. This is a persuasion not only favorable to liberty, but built upon it . . . The dissenting interests have sprung

up in direct opposition to all the ordinary powers
of the world, and could justify that opposition
only on a strong claim to natural liberty." And
even the social actionists who boggle at economic
and political freedom, defend liberties of the
mind by referring, as one of them does, to the
Protestant emphasis on liberty, "spiritual in its
roots, but which branches out into secular liberties."

Two movements, differing greatly in many
respects but originally agreeing in their accent
on freedom, are transmuted into their opposites.
One resultant is "ecclesiastical liberalism." Regardless of the merit of the intentions of the
men who comprise this party, it is implacably
hostile to the free society and destructive of individual liberty. Liberty must protect itself
against these liberals!

How has this situation come about? What
happened to Classical Liberalism? Why, and
under what illusions did the Colonial churches
and the American society they helped shape perform this kind of about-face? Why does the economic and political program "endorsed, after
long process of study and debate, by the major
American denominations, by the National Council
of Churches and by the World Council of
Churches" show symptoms of a return to the
Old Regime of privilege and despotism? To answer this question we must take a look at socialism.

The modern secular socialist movement is a
little more than a century old, and the parallel
movement in the churches is of the same vintage.
Christian socialism as a movement so named
by its founders — two Church of England clergymen, Charles Kingsley and F. D. Maurice —
dates back to 1848. Marx and Engels issued

their *Communist Manifesto* in the same year,
and although they might not have had Kingsley
and Maurice directly in mind, they scornfully
observed that "Christian socialism is but the
Holy Water with which the priest consecrates
the heart-burnings of the aristocrat."

The failure of Chartism was a factor in the
launching of Christian socialism, whose aim, in
the words of the founders, was to vindicate for
"the Kingdom of Christ (its) true authority over
the realms of industry and trade, (and) for socialism its true character as the great Christian
revolution of the 19th century." The movement
sponsored cooperatives, founded a workingmen's
college in 1854, and its influence may be traced
to the present day. A war cry of the 1880's in
England was: "Christianity is the religion of
which socialism is the practice."

The counterpart movement in post-Civil War
United States was known as the Social Gospel.
The Society of Christian Socialists was founded
in Boston in 1889 around the Reverend W.D.P.
Bliss, "To show that the aim of socialism is
embraced in the aims of Christianity." In 1908
came what C. H. Hopkins, the sympathetic chron-
icler of these movements called "The climax of
official recognition of social Christianity . . . in
the organization of the Federal Council of
Churches of Christ in America." Hopkins goes
on to say, "Not only was the social gospel acknowledged in an impressive manner by this
most representative body in American Protestant
history, but social action itself was one of the important factors that brought the Federal Council
into being." That is to say, the churchmen who
brought the Council into being did not hold doctrinal or theological convictions in common;
they formed a united front along economic and

political lines. They were Christians of various persuasions and denominations, but they were Socialists of one mind.

The movement of secular internationalism began to gather strength during this same period, and the ecumenical movement in the churches was not far behind. Various international church conferences were held, culminating in the 1948 meeting at Amsterdam where the World Council of Churches was formed. It was Amsterdam that produced the official report which so shocked many of the laity who had little or no inkling of the ecclesiastical outlook on political and economic matters. The report on The Church and the Disorder of Society declared that "The church should make clear that there are conflicts between Christianity and capitalism... The Christian churches should reject the ideologies of both communism and laissez faire capitalism, and should seek to draw men away from the false assumption that these extremes are the only alternatives."

The Christian Socialist will, of course, automatically reject "capitalism," but there is no guarantee that he will automatically understand the implications of either socialism or capitalism. As a matter of fact, he understands neither, and it is at this point that his confusion between ends and means is most evident; his means are completely out of alignment with the ends he says he wants to reach.

Socialism in the modern world has come to us under two aspects. It is, on the one hand, the vision of an ideal society from which poverty, injustice, war and ignorance have been eliminated. It is, in short, utopia — the kingdom of God on earth. The great theologian, Baron Friedrich von Huegel, writing in 1912, comments:

"For men of this mentality, a time of universal peace and plenty, of absolute equality and entire contentment, is here quite certainly to come, and quite certainly by means of the Social Revolution alone; and all this is to be here below, entirely within, entirely through, our simple human powers and earthly lives. It is a sort of Kingdom of God, but without a King and without a God."

But the utopian vision is only half of socialism, the latter half, the end, aim or goal. In some measure, all men of good will share the goal proclaimed by the Socialists. Realistically, in full awareness that imperfect human beings can never constitute a perfect human society on their own, all generous-minded men nevertheless want to see their fellows happier and better educated, enjoying more creaturely comforts and material prosperity, with nations having longer periods of international peace. It is hard to quarrel with these as desirable and desired goals. But men differ sharply when it comes to means. What practical steps, individually and socially, must we take in the economic and political sectors of life, in order to achieve these goals?

The Socialist has a ready answer: Put government in charge! More precisely, the Socialist advocates what he calls the public ownership of productive property, or of significant sectors of economic life, such as banking, transportation, communications, or mining. Now "the public," or "society" is not an entity which can exercise ownership functions; only government, society's enforcement agency can do this. In practice, therefore, socialism means the government ownership and control of the means of production (or the major means), with the consequent power of disposal over the fruits of production. Government, society's legal agency of coercion, oper-

ates society according to a master blueprint and
an overall Plan. In practice, government is
given vast and arbitrary powers over the citizenry to fit them into its master Plan, which means
cancelling the millions of private plans that men
make daily for their own lives. Government must
establish production quotas for factories, fields
and mines; it must assign men to jobs, fix their
wages, their hours of labor, and the terms under
which they may exchange. Thus men are no
longer free to make their own decisions in an
important portion of their lives — the economic
sector. They are prevented from practicing a
stewardship of worldly goods. In the free society
men may change jobs until they find one that is
congenial, with an employer they like, Or, they
may go into business for themselves. In a Planned
Society, the government becomes the main employer, and it thus acquires inordinate power
over the lives of the citizens. A few men with
unlimited power ride herd on the immense majority of men, who no longer are acknowledged
to have those Creator endowed rights which, in
a free society, gives men private sectors of
individual immunity against the invasions of
governmental power. In a word, the operational
imperatives of a Socialist order cancel out the
Socialist dream.

Christianity, on the other hand, stands for
freedom. Our religious heritage spells out logi-
cally into personal liberty in the political and
economic spheres. The God who gave us the
freedom to accept or reject Him certainly in-
tends us to be free in our relationships with other
men. Unless we are free, we cannot be responsible for the proper ordering of our souls, for
which we are accountable to our Maker. And one
of the important disciplines of freedom is the

proper stewardship of material resources. Stewardship is opposed to waste, and to violate the
rules of economics in the allocation of scarce
goods is to be guilty of wasting the planet's
resources.

Christian socialism, as such, is no longer the
live option for churchmen it once was. Reinhold
Niebuhr was a Marxian Socialist in the thirties,
confidently writing in 1935, "The program of
the Marxian will not create the millenium for
which he hopes. It merely will provide the only
possible property system compatible with the
necessities of a technical age." Despite the dogmatic assurance of this statement, Niebuhr's
mind has changed. Now, even he recognizes "that
consistent socialization or even regulation of
property unduly maximizes political power, re-
placing self-regulating tendencies in the market
with bureaucratic decisions. . ." (1953). John
Bennett, likewise, was a Socialist. Incidentally,
he chaired the commission which issued the
Amsterdam "plague on both your houses" statement quoted above. But in 1954 he repudiated
socialism without, of course, embracing any
recognizable alternative. "A thorough going collectivism," he writes, "and a thorough going
individualism are two types of economic system
the Christian can reject in advance."

What did Dr. Bennett think they were dealing
with when he and his associates rejected "capitalism" at Amsterdam? The report lists four
features of the thing they understood by "capitalism." Here are the earmarks. "(1) Capitalism
tends to subordinate what should be the primary
task of any economy — the meeting of human
needs — to the economic advantages of those
who have most power over its institutions. (2) It
tends to produce serious inequalities. (3) It has

developed a practical form of materialism in Western nations in spite of their Christian background, for it has placed the greatest emphasis upon success in making money. (4) It has also kept the people of capitalist countries subject to a kind of fate which has taken the form of such social catastrophes as mass unemployment."

The misunderstanding involved here is monumental. If this indeed be "capitalism," then the free market economy would have few if any defenders! It has defenders aplenty, however, and the philosophy is available in brilliant and substantial books for all who wish to have it. Here, a few comments must suffice. Adam Smith, in his *Wealth of Nations*, celebrated what he called "the liberal plan of equality, liberty, and justice." The economic activities of men which he explored do not take place in a vacuum, he insisted, but within a proper framework of law. Economic life was to be contained, so to speak, by a social casing composed of spiritual, ethical, legal, and prescriptive ingredients or factors. There is, in other words, an area of life beyond the market, where monetary calculation does not apply. This social framework for economic action had been worked out by the Whigs and the Classical Liberals, and Adam Smith took it for granted — as does every other free market economist. This fact has, apparently, never come to the attention of any social actionist, as indicated by Dr. Bennett's reference to "thoroughgoing individualism" above, and as a canvassing of collectivist literature reveals. Let us, therefore, emphasize the point by quoting from F. A. Hayek's great work, *The Constitution of Liberty*. "The classical argument for freedom in economic affairs rests on the tacit postulate that the rule of law should govern policy in this

as in all other spheres. We cannot understand
the nature of the opposition of men like Adam
Smith or John Stuart Mill to government 'intervention' unless we see it against this background. Their position was therefore often misunderstood by those who were not familiar with
that basic conception; and confusion arose in
England and America as soon as the conception
of the rule of law ceased to be assumed by every
reader. Freedom of economic activity had meant
freedom under the law, not the absence of all
government action. The 'interference' or 'intervention' of government which those writers opposed as a matter of principle therefore meant
only the infringement of that private sphere
which the general rules of law were intended to
protect. They did not mean that government
should never concern itself with any economic
matters. But they did mean that there were certain kinds of governmental measures which should
be precluded on principle and which could not be
justified on any grounds of expediency." (page
220)

Misunderstanding the nature of capitalism,
churchmen are unaware of how the market, with
its pricing system, operates. They are ignorant
of the disciplines of economics which guarantee
our freedoms. They have a misplaced faith in
the power of government to correct all economic
and social ills.

The free market is the only device available to
men for allocating scarce resources equitably;
its performance is so efficient and so intelligent
that it has excited the admiration of those who
have studied and understood its workings. Virtually every one of the charges that have ever
been directed against the free economy proves,
upon examination, to be aimed at a problem

caused by some misguided political interference with the free economy.

It is a proper function of government to maintain the framework of the rule of law, within which economic life functions, but when any government oversteps these bounds it inaugurates the system of privilege, it unjustly and coercively puts a portion of the lives and services of some men at the disposal of those with power. Once this point is grasped, it is obvious that every form of collectivism, from communism to the Great Society, stands in violation in one degree or another, of the second part of the Great Commandment. When our neighbor is being coerced for our benefit we are not loving him. If men should be related to one another by the ties of love, and if every collectivist society interposes relations of coercion between men, then "Christian socialism" is a contradiction in terms. And this is what the major thrust of the contemporary Great Church's involvement in politics boils down to.

There is a right way for man in each of the various departments of his personal and social life, and a vigorous pursuit of wrong ways is one method for discovering the true way. The method is not recommended, for it is roundabout and painful; but it is an experience, and it may teach.

The world-renowned Swiss economist, Wilhelm Roepke, one of the first university men chased out by Hitler, and who in recent years has been rightly credited with supplying the expertise to Mr. Erhardt for the miracle of West German economic recovery, has written movingly of his experiences fighting twentieth century collectivism, and of the horrors Europeans have lived through since 1914. "For more than a century," he writes, "we have made the hopeless effort more and more baldly proclaimed, to get along without God. . . It is as though we wanted to add to the already existing proofs of God's existence, a new and finally convincing one; the universal destruction that follows on assuming God's nonexistence." What, then, shall we do, we ask Professor Roepke. "The genesis of the malady from which our civilization suffers," he concludes, "lies in the individual soul and is only to be overcome within the individual soul."

To speak of the individual soul in this age of the revolt of the masses, makes us a little uncomfortable, even in church. Isn't the individual insignificant in a period when "great social forces are on the march?" What can the mere individual do when confronted by the power available to society? Does the individual really count any more, or is he just a unit to be counted?

Two developments in modern science may, by way of analogy, help us weigh this question: the development of atomic energy and the invention of the reaction motor. The physics of a generation ago talked about potential and kinetic energy; the force exerted was calculated in terms of mass times velocity. Hoist a one ton weight to the height of ten feet, and the kinetic energy released by its fall is considerable. But if you drop a tiny portion of that weight, a pound say, little energy is involved. Let's now ignore that one ton mass altogether and concentrate on one of its components so tiny that it cannot even be seen — the atom. We now know that there is far more energy locked up in that individual atom than in the mass of atoms comprising the one ton weight . . . dealt with *en masse!*

The individual is discarded today as a negligible factor in the planning of the politically powerful or cursed as an obstruction. But if we change our perspective we realize that the individual is the most potent force we know. Before we write him off as a mere by-product of social forces, reflect on the power in the infinitely small atom. And also on that new development called the reaction motor, where the element we tried vainly to get rid of has turned out to be the thing of highest value.

Jet travel is now commonplace. The general principle on which it is based has been known ever since the first bow and arrow, but it was Isaac Newton who first formulated the principle as his third law of motion. "To every action there is always an equal and contrary reaction." The recoil of a rifle illustrates this law; the action speeds the bullet on its way while the reaction bruises the shoulder. Coping with this reaction posed quite a problem for artillery men. John Moses Browning, the 19th century American inventor, was able to devise a way to use a portion of this force of recoil to get rid of the spent shell and move a new cartridge into place: the Browning automatic.

But now, in the reaction motor of jet engines and rockets, we have found a way to use the reaction fully. This force, which for centuries was a nuisance to people who wanted the action only, now provides propulsion by reaction which is enormously efficient in air travel, and the only means of propulsion in outer space. Even so the individual person. Social planners have always viewed him as a monkey wrench in their machinery. The precise opposite is true. Far from being a monkey wrench in the machinery, the individual is actually the key to the whole process — the only key. If he is not its end, the social process makes no sense as a means.

Part of the message of Jesus is that the Infinitely Great is concerned with the infinitesimally small. How this can be so, or why, is a mystery; but the Maker of heaven and earth cares for his creatures and solicits their fellowship. Every individual person counts because he's included in God's plan. This is why, as Christians, we resist the inordinate powers which present day government have over the lives of individuals; and this is why we must oppose the misguided efforts of some churchmen to provide these powers with religious sanction.

Harry R.
Butman

Chapter 4

The Ecumenical Movement

BUILDING A
POLITICAL KINGDOM

HARRY R. BUTMAN

Harry R. Butman was born in Beverly, Massachusetts, and educated in the public schools of that city. He attended Bangor Theological Seminary and the University of Vermont, and received a degree of Doctor of Divinity from Piedmont College. He was ordained to the Congregational ministry in 1932, and served three Massachusetts Churches (all within forty miles of Plymouth Rock) until he moved to Los Angeles, where he is presently the pastor of the Congregational Church of the Messiah.

Early in the controversy which arose over the merger of the Congregational Christian Churches and the Evangelical and Reformed Church he became active in the Continuing Congregational cause. He has been moderator of the National Association of Congregational Christian Churches, and is currently the chairman of the Commission on World Christian Relations.

His major hobbies are sailing and basketball, which he played from 1919 to 1963. He has written a number of juvenile stories, mostly on marine topics, as well as a number of articles on Congregational polity and libertarian themes. He is married and has four children and six grandchildren.

The Ecumenical Movement

BUILDING A
POLITICAL KINGDOM

by Harry R. Butman

THE PRIMACY OF POWER

The brutal reality of the building of the political church by the ecumenical movement of the twentieth century can be more precisely seen if we look at a relatively small area rather than at the whole audacious sweep of the effort to erect a global ecclesiastical empire. We shall focus attention on the way in which the Congregational Christian fellowship, a decentralized company of local Churches, has been transformed, in less than two decades, into a national body — the United Church of Christ, which frankly and proudly applies such political pressures as are at its beck, and will forward and promote its conception of the function of a Church which is in the world and of the world. The area of attention will be further narrowed by the fact that the writer will first consider only that portion of the struggle which came under his personal attention during the period 1948 to 1960 when the United Church of Christ was formed by the merger of the Congregational Christian Churches and the Evangelical and Reformed Church. But what his presentation lacks in scope it may make up in detail and intensity. This merger was the first successful step in the bold venture of constructing a super-Church in America. The importance of the

political motivation of the ecumenical movement
may be seen in solid, three-dimensional form in
the current philosophy and action of the United
Church of Christ. The naked and unashamed
craving to give the Church of Christ a place in
the power structure of a nation may nowhere be
seen with greater clarity than in this particular
segment of the total ecumenical movement.

Planners of the One Great State believe that if
education and persuasion cannot bring men to
bow to the yoke of the single sovereign aims of
the State, then force must be brought into play.
If a man will not obey the will of the State, he
must be made to do so. Planners of the One
Great Church are no more free from the logic
of power than are the framers of the One Great
State; power is the ultimate factor.

Protestants may have looked with some degree
of enthusiasm upon the high ideals of the
Ecumenical Movement as they were urged in the
days of Archbishop William Temple and Bishop
Nathan Soderblom. They were concerned with
matters of faith and order and not involved in
the demonic dream of a Church that could speak
a word of power to the nations. There is an
ecumenicity of the spirit which is valid and good;
a oneness of good will and brotherhood, a breadth
of mind and heart, and a common concern for
advancing the will of God and the salvation of the
world. But today the Ecumenical Movement has
become a militant, politically oriented ecclesiastical drive for One Great Church with massive
political power.

I am a Congregationalist. I have had reason to
see this modern movement at work in my own denomination moving from a stance of theological
idealism to one of political dynamic. It began with
an idealistic, theological and spiritual appeal for

merger of the Congregational-Christian Churches
with the Evangelical and Reformed Church.

The division of Christendom into disputing
hostile sects seemed to many to be a scandal.
I was one who held such a view. The competition
of marginal Churches in over-churched areas, the
overlapping of efforts in urban situations and on
the mission field, seemed to call for corrective
action. But very early the idealism began to be
infected by an indifference to the means by which
the great goal was to be reached.

THE CORROSIONS OF POWER

In 1948 I went to the meeting of the General
Council of Congregational Christian Churches at
Oberlin, Ohio, leaning toward merger. There I saw
the Devil's hoof thrust forth from beneath the robe
of righteousness. I saw political means used to
gain spiritual ends. I saw youth rallies being addressed by important and persuasive speakers,
but only the case for ecumenicity was presented. I
listened to hints that those pastors who did not "go
along" with the official position might find trouble
when the time came to seek another parish.

One evening, when a great rally for merger
was being held at the campus Chapel, some stirring of intellectual curiosity, some unease stem-
ming from the Congregational tradition of respect for minorities, sent me searching for a
meeting of the opposition party. I sought long and
inquired much without result. Finally I found a
group of people down in the basement of a remote
dormitory: they were standing about, or sitting
on pool tables, because there were no chairs. I
learned that the program committee for the
General Council meeting had decided it was un-
wise to provide a place of assembly for dissidents who were not in favor of the course which

a small, but powerful and articulate inner circle
of officials had decided upon. This practical
denial of the right of assembly, and the later
difficulty dissidents experienced in getting space
for their opinions in the denominational journal
and access to microphones in assembly, was un-
comfortably reminiscent of the techniques totalitarian leaders had used on their way to power

It is interesting to contrast these first tentative
uses of ecclesiastical power at Oberlin in 1948
with the radical uses of secular power proposed
by the United Church of Christ at its Fifth General Synod, held in Chicago in July, 1965, as these
proposals were reported by the *Los Angeles
Times*, from which all the following quotations
are taken. At Chicago there was an absolutely
candid avowal of the desire of the United Church
of Christ to be a part of the power structure of
the United States. There is no hedging or equivocation at this point. Dr. Ray Gibbons, director of
the United Church of Christ's Council for Christian Social Action, was emphatic in his comment
on a speech by a Kentucky coal miner who spoke
of the economic situation in Appalachia, saying:
"Our only answer is to get the political power out
of the mine operators' hands." Commented Dr.
Gibbons, "Our job is to listen to this type of
statement, and respond to it."

Dr. Gibbons warned against "Band-aid" cures for poverty
ills. What is needed, he said, is "area redevelopment and re-
gional planning, increased and extended minimum wages,
adequate and inclusive social insurance, major public works,
programs, conservation and development of natural resources, encouragement of economic growth and assurance
of basic income." The poor can be brought into the main-
stream of American society, he said, only by the achievement of economic and political power. "Until they have a
voice, organization and power to speak for themselves," he
said, "justice will not prevail."

Other statements and publications by Dr. Gibbons and members of the staff of the Council for
Christian Social Action leave no doubt but that
these officials consider the primary task of the
United Church of Christ to be the attainment of
these economic and political objectives. No Bib-
ical warrant is cited for these programs. There
are other sources of God's will, declared Dr.
Truman B. Douglass, executive vice president
of the Board of Homeland Ministries of the United
Church of Christ, and clergyman of note in the
ecumenical movement:

"The Word of God for us is sometimes in the writings of
Marx and Trotsky," he said.

At the recent convention of his church, Dr. Douglass
listened intently to the fiery, impassioned and cruel words
spoken from a Christian pulpit by an embittered young Negro
Nationalist.

"You say you love me," the Negro sneered at the congregation.

"Don't give me that bunk. I don't want your love. First
give me your respect. You say you want to help me. I don't
want your help. I'll help myself. I'll be a man — a human
being — in spite of you!"

Dr. Douglass was silent a moment as his thoughts turned
on the young man's heated statements.

"I believe," he said at last, "there was more of the Word
of God for us in the words of this Negro than in the words of
Scripture read earlier in the service."

It is not to the point here to ask by what involved process of exegesis a minister ordained
to proclaim the Gospel of One who said, "A new
commandment give I unto you, that you love one
another," is able to make these arrogant words
of hatred superior, in one instance at least, to
the words of Holy Writ. It is enough to note that
the Bible, once "a sufficient rule of faith and
practice" for Congregational ministers, can be
superseded on occasion, in the opinion of a
powerful leader of the United Church of Christ,
by a snarl of fury. But this emancipation from the

traditional ethic of Christianity is commendable in the eyes of some clergymen. Dr. Douglass agreed further on in the news report just cited, "that the United Church of Christ has become in many ways one of the most progressive of American churches."

There is something rather chilling about the bland way in which Christ and his teachings are ignored in the zeal for political power and social reform. In the *Los Angeles Times* for Sunday, July 11, 1965, there is an interview with Dr. Purd E. Dietz of the United Church of Christ. This article contains three hundred and thirty-three lines of five words each — the secular press is extremely generous in giving space to proponents of ecumenicity. With the exception of its use in the title, "United Church of Christ," the name of the Founder of the Christian Church does not appear once. John Boyle O'Reilly, a minor Boston poet of a generation ago, once metrically mocked social workers who had forgotten the inner meaning of Christian charity and did their chilly deeds of aid "in the name of a cautious, statistical Christ." Today the great Name itself is a casualty of the war on poverty as it is conducted by the highly organized Church.

With Dr. Dietz thus setting the tone, it is small wonder that lesser figures are encouraged to propose changes which would destroy the shape of the Christian Church as it is presently constituted. For example, at this same Fifth General Synod meeting, the Rev. Donald Benedict, an executive of the Chicago City Missionary Society, set forth "a drastic plan to refocus the denomination."

Mr. Benedict proposed that the church, which he said was still organized along 19th-century lines, be reconstructed around the major social issues of our day. He listed as samples of focal points for the new structure, public education in American ghettoes, housing, employment, poverty and public welfare and race relations. "These four or five issues will determine the whole future of American society," he said.

"What happens regarding these issues will depend on what we do to reform ourselves."

In justice to the General Synod it should be said that Mr. Benedict's proposal, would virtually abolish the parish structure of American Protestantism, was voted down. But trial balloons have been sent up many times, and what the "Young Turk" talks of today, the powerful church executive will implement tomorrow.

THE GOLDWATER EDITORIAL

Of the fixed intent of the leaders of the United Church of Christ to become deeply involved in political action for the furtherance of their social and economic ideals, there can be small doubt. An incident at the General Synod meeting underscores this point. Headlines tell the story succintly: "United Church of Christ Magazine Exonerated," "Synod Reaffirms Faith in Publication That Drew Complaints for Opposing Goldwater."

Briefly, the background facts are these: Republican Candidate for President, Barry Goldwater, was opposed by a number of influential men in the United Church of Christ. Among them was Dr. Howard Schomer, president of Chicago Theological Seminary. In the September, 1964, issue of the Seminary's journal, *The Register*, Dr. Schomer's lead editorial called upon readers to express their religious faith by their political action. He made a slashing attack on the Republican candidate as the voice of extremism, and in language which was itself not except from a charge of extremism. At the San Francisco Convention he declared, "No moderate voices (were) honored, but unswerving obedience to the *Leader* overwhelmed rational argument and roared tribal approval of *his* decisions on the most complex and baffling issues confronting

20th century humanity." Dr. Schomer continued, ". . . No duly-elected religious leader . . . would today dream of espousing Goldwater's archaic nationalism, his primitive economic individualism, or his specious appeal for good feeling rather than plain justice in race relations."

All of this might have been justified if printed in an independent journal of opinion. But when, on September 1, 1964, the *United Church Herald*, the official publication of the denomination, editorially declared "forthright opposition to Barry Goldwater," and pontificated that the immediate task of the Church was his defeat at the polls, another factor was put into the equation. The *United _Church _Herald* is published by the denomination; its editor is answerable to a board of the General Synod; it is not a privately-owned, independent paper. Instant resentment was aroused by this editorial. Laymen in the United Church of Christ who were Democrats as well as those who were Republicans expressed indignation. The point at issue was not the merits or demerits of Mr. Goldwater: what caused the storm was the fact that a tradition of more than a century's standing has been violated. Never before in the history of Congregationalism (and it was from the Congregational wing of the United Church of Christ that the printed objections came) had a denominational magazine opposed a presidential candidate by name. The action of the *United Church Herald* was patently political partisanship.

In California the protest was led by "The Laymen's 'Social Action' Study Group" composed of a number of prominent laymen residing mostly in Pasadena, or its environs. They had for long opposed the social action program of the Southern California Conference of the United Church of

Christ, as it was implemented and promulgated
by Dr. Julian Keiser, Conference Minister of
Social Action. Dr. Keiser's persistent advocacy
of causes counter to the convictions and consciences of this group of able laymen had led
them to send out a newsletter which drew attention to the divergences between Dr. Keiser's
philosophy and actions and the more conservative
stance of the laymen of the former Congregational Christian Churches. By no means could
these men be called wild-eyed extremists. They
were capable, highly articulate men, possessed
of a sweet reasonableness which the obduracy of
Dr. Keiser was long in overcoming. They had
remained loyal to the United Church of Christ
in the hopes that their moderate viewpoint might
in some measure alleviate what they considered
(with reason) the leftist trend of the denomination.

The "Goldwater editorial" deeply offended their
consciences. They were angry and dismayed, but
their protests were made in a rational manner,
and with an astonishing measure of temperate-
ness, considering the shock of the offense. Their
remonstrances were of no avail, of course. Although these men had been told that the hard
inner core of United Church of Christ leadership
was irrevocably committed to throw the force
of the Church behind political programs, they
were unwilling to accept this information. They
found their helplessness galling. Their request
for the removal of the editor was met with the
stock argument about editorial freedom. Realis-
tic men know perfectly well that editors do not
flagrantly oppose a general policy set by the
managing board; personal journalism is a myth
in an organization as carefully planned and
tautly run as the United Church of Christ. One

wonders if the same editorial freedom would have been granted to the editor, if by some wild chance, he had written an editorial commending Mr. Goldwater in a tone as laudatory as the September 1, 1964, piece had been excoriating.

Ten months after the episode, the General Synod formally voted to "reaffirm its confidence" in the magazine, and expressed its "faith in responsible freedom of speech and press within the United Church." What is the significance of this deliberate action long after the political issue has been buried in the dust of Mr. Goldwater's overwhelming defeat? The meaning is clear; the leaders of the United Church of Christ are serving notice that their Church, and their journal, are openly and unmistakably in the game of politics. The exonerating action of the Fifth General Synod indicates without shadow of equivocation that the editorial policy of the *United Church Herald* will be openly political, and cast in favor of the political party which most closely approximates the United Church of Christ's political posture. The United Church of Christ, like other denominations dedicated to a monolithic organizational ecumenicity, wants a place in the power structure of this nation. That power structure is political; to be of it, the Church must also be political.

To this point in our thinking we have spent much time on a tiny segment of the ecumenical movement in its particular effort to build a political church. We have limited our attention to one denomination in one of its annual meetings; we have not considered the whole scope of the ecumenical movement, nor even dealt with American efforts to organize a super-Church. This disproportion is deliberate. It will be remembered that we began with the thesis that reality might be more clearly seen if viewed intensely in a small area rather than casually scanned over a larger territory: we chose the microscopic view rather than the telescopic. But there is a further reason for our close analytical look at the United Church of Christ in action; this Church is a reality, not a blueprint. It is the first organizational success of the American ecumenicists. The leaders who fostered and brought about this merger took a calculated risk in rejecting the old family-type pattern of union, whereby the several estranged bodies of Lutherans would become reconciled, and the "separated brethren" among the Presbyterians and Methodists would compose their differences. No, this merger of the Congregationalists and the Evangelical and Reformed people was purposely planned to cross lines of dissimilar polities and divergent cultural backgrounds: it was a bold and successful experiment in denominational hybridization. Its success was in part due to the fact that laymen and pastors in general were enthralled by the vision of unity, the dream of the One. That laymen were rather naively unaware of the detailed plans with which the far-sighted ecclesiasts were prepared to bring the dream out of the clouds of contemplation into the harsh arena of political action is aside from the point. The fact of the matter is that in the United Church of Christ the observer can see the ecumenical process in action. The United Church of Christ exists; it is real. It is a strong and vivid example of the shape of things to come if organizational ecumenicity achieves the power it so ardently seeks.

ONE GREAT AMERICAN CHURCH

There is now before the American Protestant

public a proposal to unite six "mainline" denominations, with a possible ultimate membership
of twenty million. This proposal is popularly
known as the "Blake-Pike Plan" because its
most prominent proponents are Dr. Eugene Carson Blake of the United Presbyterians and Bishop
James Pike of the Protestant Episcopal Church.
The mechanism for advancing this merger is
formally known as the Consulatation on Church
Union. It meets regularly, and has come to substantial agreement on several thorny points,
notably the matter of ordination of all ministers
in the uniting Churches through the historic
episcopate. Our concern is not with the intricate
matters of orders, polity, creed, and liturgy, but
with the political orientation of the projected One
Great American Church. If the whole trend of
thought for the past twenty years in the National
Council of Churches, and in the World Council
of Churches, is any criteria of the hopes and
plans of leading American ecclesiastical figures,
the Church which emerges from the Consultation
on Church Union will be as politically focused
as the existing United Church of Christ. Indeed
there is some evidence that such is the
intent of key persons. Control of the whole
economy, it is hardly necessary to point out, is
not attainable save through political means, and
the voting impact of a twenty-million-member
Church controlled by and channeled through the
social action agencies of that Church would be of
such strength that cautious legislators would give
it respectful attention as they contemplated support or opposition to bills in which this Church
would be interested.

The pages of history are crammed with fierce
and bitter examples of what the Church has done
when its power is great. Lord Acton's famous

aphorism, "All power tends to corrupt and absolute power tends to corrupt absolutely" is as
true of institutions as of individuals. No one can
be more coldly cruel than the priest who is
certain that his cause is God's cause; to protest
his rulings is more than mere disobedience, it is
blasphemy; and no punishment is too severe for
such wickedness. I am not saying that the men
who seek to put the Church into the power structure consciously advocate, or even unconsciously
cherish, such an extreme of ruthlessness as that
which I have just described. But I do say that the
path of power on which they are setting foot has
 historically led to brutal suppression of thought,
merciless taxation, and the heretic's stake. Many
ecumenical churchmen want the Church to have
such power that when she speaks with a great
voice, the governments of this world will hear
and heed. The Church once had such a voice; but
humanity has for centuries shuddered at what
that voice said in the days of the Spanish In-
quisition.

A tragic blindness is darkening the eyes of
many Protestants, clergy and laymen alike. En-
tranced by the siren song of the extreme ecumenicist, they close their ears to the sober precepts
of history; dazzled by the sight of the One Great
Church in queenly splendor, they forget that the
really daring, the truly Christian experiment, in
the relationship of the civil and the saved, has
been made in America in the separation of Church
and State. In this land of religious freedom men
cast off the shackles of "establishment," and they
have recorded their emancipation in the first
article of the Bill of Rights. Here men have
dared to trust each other with liberty of worship;
they have not insisted on the manacles of con-
formity of conscience. The American ideal of

the separation of Church and State — belittled, excoriated, and disesteemed as that ideal now is — is a younger and a more venturesome dream than that cherished by men who would see the Church of Christ be like the kingdoms of this world. Theirs is not the forward look; rather they stare backwards toward medieval days when the Church had the power of the steel sword and the executioner's axe. The great wave of the future, which the organizational ecumenicist hopes to see rise higher and higher, is in point of sad fact the deadly undertow of the past.

It has been said that the ecumenical movement in its organizational aspects is a religious reflection of the totalitarianism of our time. But it is more than that; it has its own drive and ideology. The ecumenical Church is not a rudderless ship, chance-blown by the winds of the age. To the contrary, it follows a carefully plotted course. The direction of that course is frightening to one who holds to traditional Christianity, frightening not because of its novelty, but because it is in such radical and irreconcilable opposition to the teachings of Christ. One précis of this plan of procedure may be found in the brochure, *Where In the World,* by Dr. Colin W. Williams. Dr. Williams is Executive Director of the Department of Evangelism of the National Council of Churches of Christ, and chairman of the Department of Studies in Evangelism of the World Council of Churches; he therefore speaks as one having authority. The book is a study authorized at New Delhi by the Third Assembly of the World Council of Churches, and thus, while not an official document, may fairly be taken as an authentic indication of the direction in which the thought of ecumenical officialdom is trending.

HOSTILITY TO THE LOCAL CHURCH

The study was prepared as an answer to the question, "Is the present form of church life a major hindrance to the work of evangelism?" Briefly, but not inaccurately, the answer is a resounding, "Yes." The parish Church, presently the cornerstone of the work of the Church at large, gets savage treatment at the hands of Dr. Williams and his confreres.

His conclusion is that if the ample, the concept of the local Church centering around the homes of the members, who worship in a building erected for the purpose, and are led by an ordained minister, is totally rejected as an effective means of meeting the world's needs. The importance of the parish Church is minimized; this is "the myth of the local." People no longer "live where they live"; their true interests and major decisions lie and are made outside the home, and the Church built around residence is irrelevant to the needs of today's world. The tenacity with which men and women cling to the idea of the resident congregation is dismissed as "morphological fundamentalism." The thought behind this sonorous set of syllables is that the average church member is too rigid in his view of the morphe, or structure of the congregation; he views it with the same inflexibility with which the Biblical fundamentalist views the inerrant Word of God.

The word "structure" is a favorite word of ecumenicists, and it is liberally used in this book. Interestingly, it is not to be found in the New Testament. But the restructuring of the church life of America is a primary concern of the ecumenicists, and this concern is almost feverishly expressed. The restructuring must be around "the shapes of the world's needs." The old idea of the Church as custodian and proclaimer of a Gospel which should change the world has been abandoned. The word now is that in dialogue between the Church and the world, "the world should write the agenda." As these scholars read the New Testament, it witnesses to a "a church which takes form in the world in response to the structures of the world's needs."

Now here I must confess to an honest bewilderment. I simply cannot understand how this philosophy that the Church must totally involve itself with the world can be squared with one powerful strand of New Testament thought; namely, that the world is lost, and it was for the purpose of calling a lost world back to God that Christ was sent. It would seem, from the reading of such a book as *Where in The World* that it is the Church of Christ which is lost and not the world. Those who cry for a complete involvement of the Church with the world must do so at the cost of ignoring certain central words of Scripture. Paul says: "Now we have received, not the spirit of the world, but the spirit which is of God . . ." (I Corinthians 2:12), and he speaks elsewhere (II Corinthians 5:17-20) of the deep need for the world's reconciliation with God. James, the brother of our Lord, plainly declares that one element of pure religion is "to keep himself unspotted from the world" (James 1:27). And the words of Christ himself, taken from the very chapter in which the great text of the ecumenicists is to be found, are brutally explicit in their statement of the dichotomy of the world of men and the things of the spirit. Of his disciples Jesus says, ". . . the world hath hated them, because they are not of the world, even as I am not of the World"; lest the point be

missed, he says again, "They are not of the
world, even as I am not of the world" (John 17:14,
16). And the sovereignty of the world of flesh and
time is assigned by Christ to the Accuser of
Mankind, the Enemy: ". . . the prince of this
world cometh, and hath nothing in me" (John
14:30). There is such a thing as the abuse of
Scripture's true meaning by piling up proof texts;
but there is also such a thing as ignoring or
contravening the clear commands and warnings
of Holy Writ, and the second fault seems to me
greater than the first.

The truth being stated here is that the builders
of the organized ecumenical Church are not
haphazard in their construction; they know what
they are doing; the blueprints are precise. The
radical proposals of the Rev. Donald Benedict
at the Fifth General Synod of the United Church
of Christ were based on the principles laid down
in such a book as *Where in The World;* they were
not the personal notions of a single executive.
True, wiser and older heads spoke in defense of
the local parish: perhaps out of the prudent
realization that it is still the local congregation
which pays the bills. From the offerings taken
at these derogated local Churches comes the
money which pays the salaries of men who study
to abolish the local Church. And if this judgment
seems overharsh, it is not far from fact. This
book (and there are others like it) is brilliantly
written and full of sharp incisive phrases; it is
a scalpel, keen and glittering, which, if words
become deeds, will perform such heavy surgery
upon the Body of Christ as we have seen and
known it, as will leave that beloved Body unre-
cognizable.

One finds himself wishing that amid the fanfare
of headlines, the turbulent drama of civil rights

participation, the push for a place in the power structure, that other sounds could be heard and other sights seen. How grateful would be the ears which heard, not the tuckets and flourishes and intricate orchestrations of great gatherings and corporate undertakings, but a simple straightforward tune, singing the worth of ethical behavior, the quiet glory of the inner walk with God. And how blessed would be the eyes who saw, not the Christ of Byzantine splendor and Roman might, his robes stiff with brocade, his crown of pomp gleaming, ruling the world with power; but the Man of Nazareth, walking the ways of this present time as he walked road and lakeshore in the days of his flesh, calling all who would to follow him to a Kingdom which is not of this world.

T. Robert
Ingram

Chapter 5

How Deep and Wide is

SOCIALISM

IN THE SANCTUARY?

T. ROBERT INGRAM

T. Robert Ingram was ordained in the Episcopal Church in 1950.

Previously, he had worked on daily newspapers in Denver, Honolulu and Boston. He was sent to Europe by the *Boston Globe* in 1948 as staff correspondent, between semesters of study at the Episcopal Theological School in Cambridge, Massachusetts.

During World War II, he served with the U.S. Navy and was at the assaults on Palau and Okinawa.

He has founded two successful parochial schools and has promoted church schools generally by the writing of a pioneer work in elementary school sacred studies.

He is author of a number of books and pamphlets dealing with temporal problems viewed in the light of the sovereignty of Christ. His most recent work is a study of the Ten Commandments as the basis of criminal and civil law in the United States and other Christian nations, entitled *The World Under God's Law*.

Mr. Ingram presently is Rector of St. Thomas' Episcopal Church and School in Houston, Texas.

How Deep and Wide is

SOCIALISM
IN THE SANCTUARY?

by T. Robert Ingram

The characteristic points of catholic Christian doctrine, reaffirmed in American Puritanism, which socialism refutes and seeks to displace, are listed side by side:

Christian Doctrine	*Socialism*
1. God is sovereign.	1. Man is sovereign.
2. God is revealed fully in the Bible.	2. The Bible is a human document, and unreliable.
3. Church has official guardianship of the Scriptures and of teaching them.	3. The state regulates and controls all education.
4. A Divinely endowed quality of man is the power of personal ownership of goods and cattle, given in the Dominion command to have dominion over the earth.	4. No man may rightly own anything; all goods are held "in common," which means state ownership of all property.
5. Every man may have one wife living, as ordained by God in the beginning, and the	5. No man is entitled to a wife or a family; women are held "in common," which

two become a family which is the structural unit of society.

6. The foundation of law is the commandments of God, given in Scripture.

7. The world has been corrupted by human sin; redeemed man is in the world but not of it, living in Paradise where he is restored to communion with God but awaiting complete transformation and eternal life in Heaven.

8. God created everything as set forth in Scripture.

means women belong to the state, and breed for the state.

6. Self-defense is the first law of life: *Salus populia suprema lex*

7. The world is in a mess, but it's all we have and man's task is to himself redeem the world and make it a better place; this is the socialist dream of "utopia."

8. Nature, and therefore man as supreme in nature, is self-made. The process is called evolution and aeons of time are necessary to explain it.

EDITOR'S NOTE

You may be aided in judging how far Socialism has penetrated your church or your denomination by critically listening, reading or just watching.

LISTEN to the sermons; the invited speakers; the discussions by the members.

READ the Sunday School literature; your church

*paper; your denominational newspaper or maga-
zine.*

*WATCH for material from the National Council
of Churches; the pronouncements of policies; the
selection of committees and delegates.*

*The following brief discussion is designed to help
you judge the degree of penetration by enlarging
on the above points or characteristics.*

1

Surely there is no catholic doctrine more certain or more fundamental than the sovereignty
of God. The obverse of this doctrine, equally
certain, is that the mystery of iniquity is the
passion of ascribing sovereignty to human kind.
The Beast of the Apocalypse of St. John has a
mysterious number which John tells us "is the
number of a man." St. Paul says the man of sin,
the son of perdition, "opposeth and exalteth
himself above all that is called God, or that is
worshipped; so that he as God sitteth in the
temple of God, shewing himself that hie is God."

If there is any characteristic of the Puritan or
Calvinist system, accorded even by its foes, it is
that all turns around this principle of God's
sovereignty. "The Lord," says Isaiah, "is our
judge; the Lord is our lawgiver; the Lord is our
king." The rejection of kingship in the United
States was largely in recognition of what New
Englanders called "the crown rights of King
Jesus." Adams rebuked the southern leaders for
talking about state sovereignty, not because he
saw it in the central government, but because it
belonged only to God.

It does not seem necessary for the purpose
here to spell out even the major doctrines that
flow both politically, personally and religiously

from the sovereignty of God and its corollary
that evil is the ascription of sovereignty to man.
It is plain enough that it is the Rock upon which
the Christian religion rests, and which must at
least be presupposed as the basis of all other
teachings. It is equally plain that socialism
begins by rejecting God as sovereign, although it
may seek to admit Him as a kind of ideal or
abstraction of reality, and by attempting to establish a seat of sovereignty which will be in this
world and will be *a* man.

What we call "world government" means just
that: it means a seat of absolute power in human
hands to which all other power and authority
becomes subject. If Christians do not understand
that world government is incompatible with the
sovereignty of God, the Socialists do. They know
world government can come only when the present order is overthrown. They therefore begin
and end as "revolutionists." Everything that re-
volts or overthrows established order is counted
as good. That man can mount a revolution against
God's order seems to ascribe a kind of independence and sovereignty to man, but it cannot be
fully realized until all trace of the Divine establishment is clean gone. Christians are often
misled by fixing their eyes on one particular
scheme for world government as bad, whereas
socialism looks far beyond: it looks to the seat-
ing of sovereignty anywhere as long as it is in
the hands of a man. The alternative Socialists
say is anarchy, because they deny God is sovereign really.

Does it not follow that socialism has penetrated
Christian teaching to the extent that men and
women and children in churches, in Sunday
Schools, in school, in the newspapers, in the lecture hall, in the theater and over the radio and

television are bombarded with advocacy of world government?

James Paul Warburg proclaimed the socialist position unabashedly before the United States Senate on February 17, 1950. He is reported as saying, "We shall have World Government, whether World Government will be achieved by conquest or consent."

This is a skillful and effective offensive tactic. The issue of the war is stated as no longer in doubt: the only question is whether Christians will give in peaceably and consent to socialism, or whether it will be forced upon them. Seemingly no one is troubled about whether we shall have world government at all in Warburg's sense. There is no sound of the Christian claim that we already have true World Government, and that it is seated in the person of the Living Lord Jesus Christ. That Warburg could make such a boast before a body representing the war making powers of this people dedicated to the sovereignty of God is perhaps the best measure we have of socialist penetration of religious thinking.

A statement from the *Adult Student Sunday School Quarterly* of the Methodist Church, for example, has a strong flavor of UN support *as a possible world government:* "Ours is a divided world. We are trying desperately to find some common base in the United Nations. This will be a great day for the church if it can rise to the need of mankind and manifest a new and spiritual unity."

2

The Methodist Sunday School material cited above provides a fine example of what was happened here. First, notice that it is necessary in this material even now to assume what is said

here about Scripture: "It is our mandate from
the Church (sic!) to keep the Bible alive, free to
work miracles in the hearts of men — to make
true 'Bible Christians' saturated with the spirit
of the Bible, dominated by the message of the
Bible, guided by the purpose of the Bible." This
in October, 1962.

But now let us see how the Bible is dealt with
actually in the same set of material: "The Evan-
gelists were so eager to prove Jesus' messiah-
ship, they almost denied his manhood, giving the
impression from time to time that he was not
fully human." "Other New Testament writers
come into sharp conflict with one another." "The
documents were produced by the church as the
need arose." "It ought to be evident that any attempt to interpret this great book as a prediction of world history in general, either back in
the Old Testament period or down into modern
times, only introduces hopeless confusion and
gets entirely away from the author's meaning."
"Paul was mistaken." "In this he (Jesus) was
entirely mistaken." ". . . since there was no
Church at the time, he (Jesus) could hardly have
spoken thus."

The Methodist material is no exception; it is
typical of what is offered today from the seminaries and the pulpits as well as in schools of
all descriptions. We may say it is the general
evaluation of Scripture. There is no need to raise
the question of Genesis 1, since the above quotations have to do with the basic estimation of the
New Testament. Genesis 1, however, stands like
an immovable rock upon which rests the whole
matter of credibility of Scripture: if it falls, the
whole structure falls. But where this account of
Creation stands in religious circles today may
be understood from some of the frantic efforts

made in circles that call themselves "fundamentalist" to reconcile Genesis 1 with the supposed truth of evolution.

It would be rash indeed even to guess at how
far this basic assumption of the unreliability of
Scripture has gone in all religious circles. It
may be noted, however, that the work of Dr.
Henry Morris, a hydraulic engineering professor,
and Dr. John C. Whitcomb, a seminary Bible
professor, is rated by the Banner of Truth Trust
in England as "epoch making." Morris and Whitcomb have advanced the thesis, with an overwhelming accumulation of data and analysis, that
the Biblical record accommodates the scientific
data far better than any evolutionary theory and
is a fully reliable guide for interpreting that
data. Their thesis is startling, to say the least;
but 100 years ago would have been the generally
accepted view.

3

The role of the Church as the guardian of Holy
Writ is so well established that even the Methodist Sunday School material takes note of it as
quoted above, albeit with a marvelous strange
application. The implications of the catholic
position that the Bible is God's revelation of
Himself to man, and that the Church is the guardian and interpreter of it, are two-fold: 1) Scripture is the subject of all learning; 2) the Church
is the official teacher of the community. Obviously Scripture, where it is not regarded as wholly
and literally true, the Divinely inspired body of
knowledge given to man, cannot be the subject
matter of education. It seems equally obvious that
if Scripture is rejected as the substance of doctrine, another official teacher must be found.
Insofar as this has taken place, socialism has

penetrated religious education.

Fortunately we have irrefutable evidence by which we can take our measure. No lengthy documentation is needed. First is the fact that the content of schooling in Colonial America was Scripture: today the Supreme Court has ruled that the Bible may not be taught. Secondly, the Church has been all but displaced by the State as the official teacher.

When Augustine of Hippo wrote his brilliant treatise on Christian doctrine, he assumed straight off that the subject matter was Scripture. He devotes himself to a discussion of how one learns the Scripture so as to qualify as a teacher, and then how to go about teaching it. He does not shrink from the "extremist" implications of his view, and holds that no learning is of value that does not contribute to an understanding of Scripture.

We should hasten to point out here for the comfort of timid Christians that Augustine was not a man of limited intellect, and his system did not train men of limited intellects. Despite the calumnies of the moderns against past centuries, an honest mind can only stand in subdued awe before the power of Christian culture and the extent of it. Augustine is credited with having laid the foundations for what today is called "Western Civilization," and the range of his thought surpasses all but that of men like Paul of Tarsus. Like Paul, he simply had the grace and the mental power to see that the foolishness of God is greater than the wisdom of men.

Puritan America not only agreed with Augustine but tried to follow his precepts. William Kailer Dunn, in his book *"What Happened to Religious Education?"* says: "The textbooks of colonial times bear eloquent testimony to the preponderance of religious instruction . . . 'the average schoolboy had only a catechism or primer, a Psalter, and a Testament or Bible. For Latin students this list would have to be extended, but ordinarily it comprised all a boy ever used as long as he attended school.' "

Then, quoting studies by Dr. John A. Nietz of the Department of Education at the University of Pittsburgh, he says: " 'Several studies show that the early textbooks in several fields devoted much space to religion, with such emphasis declining after 1850 and nearly disappearing in some fields after 1900. For example, Robinson found that the readers used in the colonies prior to 1775 devoted 85% of the space to religion, and 8% to morals; those between 1775 and 1825, 22% to religion and 28% to morals, those between 1825 and 1875, 7.5% to religion and 23% to morals; and those between 1875 and 1915, only 1.5% to religion and 7% to morals.' "

This study is revealing of many things, and not complete without mention that by 1950 there was no trace of either religion or morals to be found in textbooks anywhere, and in the Metropolitan area referred to as Greater New York in 1950 the fact was so generally recognized and sufficiently deplored that an experiment was undertaken in the schools of Montclair, N. J. to see if some morals could not be taught. The experiment seemed to be largely just that — a laboratory exercise by some psychologists who neither had any morals or cared about teaching them.

It is also not complete without recognizing that religion and morals — namely the Bible — have been replaced with the hoary Pagan dogmas of socialism. Sometimes this is a conscious revival of Pagan culture (Classical), sometimes it is brazenly revolutionary, antinomian and Marxian. But it is all essentially the system of religious thought popularly known as socialism.

It is important to note that the big change was made after 1850. This was soon after the writings of Marx and Darwin swept Christendom; it coincides with equally startling changes in the character of public writings and speeches noted by Miss Verna Hall in her exhaustive study; and it marks the high water of the spread of the "Massachusetts System" of state schools until the Reconstruction Period after the Civil War when it was extended by right of conquest to a reluctant Christian South. It was not, in fact, until after World War I that the compulsory school attendance laws were made uniform in all the states and tightened up pretty much to their present limit. It was in the same era that socialist dogma flooded the school rooms in such things as the notorious "Rugg" texts.

Here we see the second public testimony to the penetration of socialism into religious education — the displacement of the Church as teacher by the State. The fact is noted (with apparent satisfaction and approval) by the *Encyclopedia Britannica:* "Thus the 19th century saw the final working out of the idea that the state should be substituted for the church as the official agent of education."

That this substitution is a cornerstone of the Marxian dream should hardly need to be stated. The Tenth Point of Karl Marx's *Communist Manifesto* was a demand for state schools: "Free education for all children in public schools. Abolition of children's factory labor in its present form. Combination of education with industrial production . . ." etc., etc. When Randolph Churchill was twitted by reporters in Colorado

Springs about British socialism, he retorted that
for all that Britian had nothing as socialistic as
the American public school system. And an
avowed organizer of violent revolution was quoted
by name in the Houston Post on July 10, 1965:
"Of course, I'm not a Marxist. But I will accept
certain things out of Marxism. Out of the *Communist Manifesto* I accept the public school system and a graduated income tax."

Finally, the text book study helps dramatize
the progress of socialist penetration of religion
and shows that the falling away takes place in
stages. It does not all happen at once. One of
the most symptomatic of these stages is the
spurt of interest in morals as over against
"religion." When Christian doctrine is watered
down, morals leap to the fore — for a brief
period. The popular attitude is, "I don't care
what a man believes, just as long as he doesn't
do anything wrong." The morals emphasis, however, is but a speedily passing phase in the
degeneration. Soon both morals and religion are
clean gone.

4

One facet of socialism is so characteristic
that it gives its name to it as communism. It is
the passion to strip man of his endowed powers
of ownership — what the writers of the later 18th
century called the right endowed by the Creator
upon every human being to property. The means
proposed to accomplish this dehumanizing of the
race is called "holding all goods in common,"
or the "common ownership of goods." Presumably, all own everything. But the corollary of
this is that no one owns anything. Such communism as existed in monasticism frankly recognized
this — common ownership means taking the vow

of poverty — to own nothing.

I leave it to the reader to think how thoroughly religious education is now given over to preparing people to accept, yea to advocate, government ownership of all property. Nationalization schemes are but a small, though spectacular, aspect. Dwelling places, water, food supplies — all these are within reach of the ownership by the state. It is supposedly a moral teaching that to uphold the right of ownership is in fact the vice of "greed" and malice. Irresponsibility is put forth as a virtue to oppose the sin of "selfishness."

Government regulation is a form of confiscation. It is true that it is lawful for me to do what I will with mine own: what I may not do with as I will is not mine own. Another person and his goods are not mine own and I may not infringe upon either.

5

Islam offers another instructive illustration of the second great characteristic of socialism — community of wives. Plato advised it; the Moslems attempted it. Their expedient was the harem. Since these actions proceed in phases, however, we cannot lay the end result in the Mohammedan world against present day pressures to make comparisons. We must keep in mind that in no case that we know of has the Platonic dream come true. It always has to stop with make-shift arrangements. The commune system of modern China has already been severely restricted, as it was earlier in Bolshevik Russia and seems to be in the state of Israel. But a terrifying and often devastating strain is put upon family life in all cases. It is, after all, the Biblical ideal of the family that is under attack. Any means to that end is a step along the path to socialism's utopia.

Much has already been done to that end in the United States. The widespread revision of marriage and divorce laws in the 1920's was perhaps the greatest single step. The present phase, however, seems to call for a new penetration of family life by mounting an assault of what Moses called the doctrine of Balaam — a destruction of the most basic sexual morality. It is in just this area that the greatest shockers are coming to Christian people today in the name of Christian education.

The propaganda line is simple, like any advertising slogan. It is simply that sexual relationships are pure and moral as long as the parties involved are "in love;" marriage vows are irrelevant. The much touted "pill" that guards against pregnancy is advertised with crude subtilty by preachers who ask their youth groups to discuss what effect the pill has on their attitude toward sex. Love is frankly taught as being something that may exist between any two persons under any conditions, even so as to make homosexuality perfectly acceptable. When a Suffragen Bishop of Texas heard a speech on that vein given to a convention of Episcopalian young people, he was astonished; and when he reported it to the House of Bishops, they paid no attention to him, refusing to believe it, really. But there is no excuse for surprise: this has been going on for years, although not as openly and as brazenly as at the moment. The National Council of Churches booklet on the subject, *"Called to Responsible Freedom,"* (1961), treats the matter in this way and any interested person can learn more than he will want to hear if he will simply take the trouble to read the material being disseminated in the name of the churches among young people everywhere. The Platonic corollary that babies belong to the state is inescapable. Parents merely breed. The family, instituted of God and reaffirmed by Jesus, is thus thoroughly corrupted, and the Christian order that much more nearly overthrown. Planned Parenthood is a spearhead in this maneuver, and is almost universally approved outside of official Roman Catholic Dogma. Efforts to legislate the Roman teaching away speak for themselves.

6

The next point of Christian teaching to be considered for evidence of Socialist penetration is that the law is God's law, specifically the Ten Commandments; that crime is a violation of this law; and that civil magistrates serve as God's ministers to punish criminals. It is clear where such is the accepted principle of civil government that it is a violation of the law for civil magistrates to use the force of the community to accomplish anything more. To use it to regulate industry, commerce and agriculture, for example, is to invade the rights to property which it is commissioned to uphold by punishing all infringements.

One of the strongest claims of Christians in the Middle Ages in their attempts to convert Jews was that it was in Christendom alone that the Ten Commandments were the law of the land. The great English legalist, William Blackstone, based his famous legal commentary on the principle that the law is imbedded in nature as created by God, and that while it might be discovered by human reason, human reason must bow before Scripture in the determination of the law. Common law, the law common to every person in the realm, is this law of God.

The alternative to this, offered in socialism and Paganism, is that the state is the seat of all power, and that all law is whatever the state decrees. The fundamental principle of such law is expressed by the Romans in the phrase *salus populi suprema lex*. The defense of the realm is the first law of the land. This is the Machiavellian principle. It is perfectly expressed in its rationale and meaning by an American educator, one of the chief advocates of the state school system, James G. Carter, in 1824. "As the first object in the formation of every government is to provide for its own preservation; and as the general diffusion of knowledge and virtue is the most effectual, if not the only means of insuring stability to republican institutions, the policy of the liberal appropriations made by Congress for education, in every new state they incorporate, is undoubtedly an enlightened policy, and worthy of an enlightened and free government."

That this theory of government has penetrated religion throughout Christendom, and thereby religious education, is sadly enough beyond question. It is so much the case that it is very difficult for most people today even to imagine what is involved in the system of law that prevailed in the United States until after World War I, despite the ravages of the preceding century.

On the other hand, teaching on the law is next to impossible to find in any religious circles. H. G. Herklots, in a socialistic treatment of the Ten Commandments, notes that no major work has been published in the field for 50 years. Silence about the law of God as the law of the land is the full realization of the socialist dream at least in this regard. Yet the law is the very subject matter .of Christian teaching, the "school-master to lead us unto Christ."

Christianity Today in April, 1963, published a piece seeking to reestablish the law, the Old Testament, as the subject matter for Christian study — the guide from Heaven for sanctification! Yet it was clearly a lonely voice in defense of the Scripture as the learning given to man to which he is to devote his whole energy all his days.

7

Probably no surer single gage of socialism is given than the passion for "utopia." This contrasts sharply and unreconcilably with the Christian passion for heaven: "Pie in the sky," in socialist mockery. The end of anything may be defined as that which justifies any means the end therefore controls all that precedes it. The judgment of Jesus Christ is the end of the world, according to all Christian doctrine. According to socialism, the end of the world, the goal toward which all is directed, is a better world than the one God has put us into. Martin Buber, Jewish scholar, goes to some pains to establish convincingly that Marxism is a thoroughgoing utopianism, and *therefore is a true respresentative of the socialist family*. Both ends cannot meet. Where the end is utopia, it is no heaven and the Gospel has given way to socialism.

Again, quotations may be taken at random from Sunday School material to document the fact that children are being taught they should devote their lives to this world rather than to heaven. But such teaching is so universal today that it would be endless and boring to belabor the case. Anyone who does not seek a better world stands condemned already in religious circles.

8

Just as ends determine the means for all things, so are the ends of all things in the beginnings, and we could not conclude this analysis without taking note of the contrast between the Christian belief in Creation as recorded in Genesis 1, and the socialistic belief in evolution. It is sad that so few people today are mentally equipped to see the difference. Suffice it to say there is no warrant for presuming to better a world that God made: therefore it must be raucously maintained that nature is self creating. Or, to parody the Psalm, "It is not He that hath made us, but we ourselves." There neither has been produced conclusive scientific evidence to support evolution, nor any adequate weight of reason. Scripture cannot be twisted to accommodate it in any form. Yet it was seized upon hungrily, almost ravenously, by intellectuals in the mid-19th century who had already long since given themselves over to seeking utopia instead of heaven. Charles Darwin seemed to provide what they had to have to support the whole business: scientific evidence for self-creation. The famous funeral oration over the body of Karl Marx, delivered by his patron and co-worker, Friedrich Engels, stressed the point. He said, "Just as Darwin discovered the law of evolution in organic nature, so Marx discovered the law of evolution in human history." Men wanted to believe it so badly that they refused then and now to be swayed by the fact that Darwin's essential theories, like those of every other systematic evolutionist, have long since been exploded by other evolutionists — to say nothing of Christian thinkers. They go right on extolling Darwin for his "great contribution," which was simply that he threw a facade of scientific respectability behind the Pagan religious belief in evolution long enough to drown out objecting, and too often uninstructed, cries of Christians.

Today the question about the teaching of evolution is not even whether it is taught everywhere as fact: that much was admitted many times in a controversy in California in 1964. The only question now is whether Christian boys and girls have to learn it in socialist school systems in violation of their professed religious beliefs. In California it was frankly stated that would mean complete replacement of most of the textbooks to clean them up of the teaching of evolution as a fact — not simply books on science, but history, literature, geography and even many first grade readers.

The extent to which evolution has acceptance from the pulpit, the Sunday School, and the seminary is a depressing measure of the extent of penetration of socialism into all education which, in Christian life, is wholly religious.

Wilbur G.
Williams

Chapter 6

SOCIALIST PENETRATION
OF RELIGIOUS
EDUCATION MATERIAL

WILBUR G. WILLIAMS

Reverend Wilbur G. Williams has been active in printing and publishing of Sunday school lesson material for the last several years. After completing work on his M.S. degree at Butler University in Indianapolis, Indiana, where he majored in Religious Education, he spent a year in England in 1958/59 at Manchester University doing graduate research.

In 1959 he returned to the States to become Editor of the Higley Press which at that time published two complete lines of Sunday school literature, and two Sunday school lesson commentaries.

Reverend Williams is presently working towards his doctorate at New York University; he received his M.A. degree there in 1965. He is also Editor of the Evangelical Sunday School Lesson Commentary, whose circulation has doubled since he took over the position six years ago. He was ordained in the Wesleyan Methodist Church and has also had seven years of pastoral experience. He also preached extensively in England.

In connection with his work Reverend Williams has had many occasions to study Sunday school quarterlies and numerous other church periodicals, pamphlets, and publications at close range. He has watched the rapid decline in the quality of religious education literature, due in large part to the wholesale embrace of socialistic schemes and goals. This chapter is an outgrowth of his research.

SOCIALIST PENETRATION
OF RELIGIOUS
EDUCATION MATERIAL

by Wilbur G. Williams

Thirty-five years ago a procedure was decided upon in the Lenin School of Political Warfare to effect total Communism the world over. The speaker was Dimitry Manuilsky, and his words were,

"War to the hilt between Communism and Capitalism is inevitable. Today, of course, we are not strong enough to attack. Our time will come in 20 to 30 years. To win we shall need the element of surprise. The bourgeoisie will have to be put to sleep. So we shall begin by launching the most spectacular peace movement on record. There will be electrifying overtures and unheard of concessions. The Capitalist countries, stupid and decadent, will rejoice to cooperate in their own destruction. They will leap at another chance to be friends. As soon as their guard is down, we shall smash them with our clenched fist."

Here we have the goal of communism concisely stated and strategically defined. In the years since its utterance it has not been altered. There have been treaties designed for treachery, walls built for bondage, and wars fought for conquest, but more deadly, and in many ways more effective, has been the subversive tactics employed by the Communists to get us "to cooperate" in our "own destruction."

Knowing that from the inception of our country the Church and the Sunday school have had a persuasive influence on the warp and woof of our successful free enterprise system, the Com-

munist set about to synthesize socialistic dogma
with Christian doctrine. Needing mouthpieces to
trumpet a "new interpretation" of Christian concepts, Socialist theoreticians found many pliant
colleagues within the ministerial circle whose
favorite motif was the Social Gospel.

Over twenty years ago Earl Browder, while
still head of the Communist Party in the United
States, appeared before the students of the Union
Theological Seminary in New York City, boast-
ing in the course of his remarks, "You may be
interested in knowing that we have preachers,
preachers active in churches, who are members
of the Communist Party."

This was no idle brag for on March 26, 1947,
Mr. J. Edgar Hoover testified before the House
Committee on Un-American Activities,

"I do fear for the liberal and progressive who has been
hoodwinked and duped into joining hands with the Communists. I confess to a real apprehension so long as Communists are able to secure ministers of the Gospel to promote
their evil work and espose a cause that is alien to the religion of Christ. . ."

One only has to read the works of some more
prominate ministers to determine that the subversive goal of fusing Christian doctrine with
socialistic dogma has had a great degree of success, unfortunately at the expense of the former
and to the advantage of the latter. Dr. Nels F.
Ferre, abbot professor Andover Newton Theological School since 1957 and a leading spokesman
who has appeared on many National Council of
Churches programs, writes,

"If Marxism should conquer the whole world, this might
be merely the prelude in economic arrangement to the
blossoming forth within it of the deeply sowed seed of Christian faith and expectations. Marxism may be God's means to
Christian fulfillment in history."

Does Dr. Ferre welcome the Communist con-

quest of the world? Students could not be blamed
if they assume that he helps advance it since
he asserted "For the common good the distribution of the rewards of society ought to be from
each according to his ability, to each according
to his need." Dr. John C. Bennett, long a prominent professor of the Union Theological Seminary
has asserted,

"Why must they conclude that there is a conflict between
Christianity and Communism?. . . certainly we cannot find
the difficulty in the Communist economic system or in Communist social goals. There is much overlapping between
Communist goals and Christian goals."

The results of Dr. Ferre and Dr. Bennett's
teachings is the dilution of Christianity as a
concession to communism. More subtle, however,
and in some ways more damaging, is the attempt
by many leaders in certain churches to undermine freedom, the pillar of democracy, and in
the void inject the inoculum of socialism. The
concept of freedom is far too strong a serum to
be overcome by simple injections of socialism;
so the former must be weakened, and this is done
by a changing of concepts, a twisting of terms,
and a variation of values.

For example, individualism is the principal
component of freedom and must be sacrificed on
the altar of mass society. How unfortunate then
to discover that one like Lewis B. Smedes,
Associate Professor of Bible at Calvin College,
who admits that he is "vigorously opposed to
Communism" and believes collectivism is a
"false religion," will yet assert,

"Individualism is a denial of the nature of man. It is a
seedbed of the suppression of individuals who are poor and
weak for the sake of the unconditioned freedom of those who
are rich and strong."

The mistake Dr. Smedes makes is to equate

individualism with selfishness, a selfishness that
would cause any special interest group to violate
the rights of others. But to make selfishness
synonymous with individualism is to mouth the
Communist line, for nowhere in the endless and
verbose verbiage of the collectivists can there
be found any station for the individual. As has
been pointed out in *What We Must Know About
Communism* by the Overstreets,

> "It is no accident that the human being in all his vital
> stubborn identity is absent from Communist writings. He has
> no place in these because he has no place in either the
> ideology or the program of Communism."

Individualism is primarily a spiritual concept;
without it a person is unable to find himself.
Jesus repeatedly geared His message to elicit
individual response, for He knew that no people
are stronger than the excellence of the members
who personify it; no society can advanve unless
there is improvement in the individuals who
comprise it.

Notice how Dr. Smedes makes individualism
the cause for "the suppression of individuals."
Does he close his eyes to socialism's slavery, a
collectivism which by its inherent nature must
refulate, prohibit, and compel?

Again in *What We Know About Communism*
we read:

> The very qualities which make him (the common man) thus
> an individual render him unfit for Party purposes. He is too
> likely . . . to look skeptical at the wrong time; to become
> bored with reiterated abstractions; to have qualms about
> methods; to hold to an opinion even after the official line
> has been reversed; to resist the pressures of Party dis-
> cipline; and, not least, to like and dislike people without
> permission from the Central Committee. He is, therefore,
> 'unreliable.' He has either to be 'developed' or else left
> as part of the 'mass' that will, when the Party fulfills its
> 'historic mission,' be dealt with according to 'proletarian
> justice.'"

Collectivism then is rather the "seedbed of the suppression of individuals," for it grimly tries to destroy the uniqueness of personality, the quality of single worth, and the attribute of individual variety.

Again in the same *Reformed Journal*, Henry Stob, Professor of Ethics and Apologetics, Calvin Theological Seminary declares,

"The effect of. . . individualism is to destroy community and to pulverize society. It breaks the community up into separate discrete particulars, each of which goes its own way. This does not mean that some sort of community is not desired; but it does mean that community is believed to issue naturally, in an unplanned fashion, by each member of it going his independent way. But the belief is false. Individualism never yields community; it only rends the fabric of society and issues into nihilism."

Where this educator stubs his toe is in equating freedom with license. Every individual was meant to be free, enslaved by neither his fellow not his State, but also to express that freedom, not in an "unplanned fashion," as Mr. Stob asserts, but with an accountability that is aware of responsibility to God and to fellowmen, knowing that if the latter is not served and the former is not honored, misery, suffering, and enslavement will result. The only alternative Dr. Stob is here presenting to individualism is what Frank S. Meyer calls, "the subtler, quieter tyranny of 'customarily' imposed community, in which no one can escape from the deadly environment of hereditarily or geographically imposed association." Such a choice, furthermore, "is vicious because it is directed to enlisting our repugnance to modern statism in behalf of a gentler tyranny."

In the April-June 1951 "Crossroads," a Presbyterian quarterly, one finds words of praise for Communism, Chinese style.

"Military might alone cannot destroy an idea of such
humanitarian appeal, for the yearnings and aspirations of
the human soul are not quieted by force. . . The Chinese
have rejected our American concept of democracy. Americans, however, should not be too shocked that our ideology
has been rejected by Communist China. The removal of the
American flag from our institutions in China is no proof
that the Christian flag has been lowered."

But where is the proof that the Christian flag
still flies? Every indication is that it has not
only been lowered, but torn to shreds. Church
buildings are now hollow museums, missionary
activity is prohibited, Christian worship is for-
bidden, and Bibles are banned. Yet great praise
is heaped upon the "Chinese Church" for devel-
oping "Christian communities" where "members
live together as a Christian family, holding
everything in common."

Such Christianization of communism is always
doomed to failure. Evil is not improved by a thin
whitewashing of the Good. Chinese Christians are
to be pitied for having to tolerate such oppression, not praised for trying to Christianize it.
In the 2nd and 1st century B.C. the Essens attempted holding "all things in common," but
they apparently did not survive the Roman conquest of 70 A.D. Very likely the archeologist
shovel will soon prove that the futile attempt at
communization in the Jerusalem church was an
outgrowth of pressures resulting from Essens
who converted to Christianity rather than return
to orthodox Judaism, and who unfortunately
brought some of their outmoded methods of
living with them.

A publication which represents an official
study authorized by the 1960 assembly of the
American Baptist Convention entitled, "Christians Face the Total Menace of Communism,"
is in many ways a commendable study, but its

subtle flaws tend to weaken its good intention. We read,

"Communism, in advocating some ideals that correspond to the Christian position, serves as a judgment on nations that claim to be Christian but have fallen down in meeting some of the crucial demands of Christian faith and morality."

Communism might feasibly be a judgment on churches who through rapprochement with corrupt systems of thought have modified their message until it lacks the healing of heart change, but what ideals of this code of evil could possibly correspond to the historic Christian position? In a kingdom-of-heaven society brought about by political and economic programs one discovers a fusing of Communist and quasi-Christian goals; however, the true religion that bears Christ's name does not contain ideals that can be achieved by human instrumentality which is oblivious of divine intervention.

Later on in that study, the leanings are less disguised in that it desires "a new kind of society" where "material things will no longer be objects which men competitively seek for themselves."

The polar points of economics are free competition and State control. Eliminate the one and you must embrace the other. But basic here is the misunderstanding that is representative of all critics of free enterprise — that it is competition for selfish reasons. A man cannot ignore the needs of others in his competitive business and succeed. The whole purpose of competition is to better determine the need of others, improve the products, and lower the costs.

In the *Methodist Youth Quarterly* of 1961 the lesson for September 10, concerned, "The Christian Citizen in International Affairs," and was given primarily to an unreserved and unre-

stricted support of the United Nations: unreserved because the only "limitation" the writer
mentions is in that "it still does not have any
jurisdiction over China"; unrestricted in that
he calls for achieving "a new world of law and
order" through UN, "even if it means surrender-
ing a measure of our national 'sovereignty.'"

Unfortunately for the youth who read the quarterly, the writer did not mention on what foundation the "law and order" was to be based. Would
it be according to the tribal law of the African
Jungle? Would a man have four wives as the
Moslems? Would murder, rape, and robbery be
legitimate as long as it advanced the cause of
the State as in Russia? Would the firing squad
be used to effect the elimination of political op-
ponents as in Cuba?

The writer of this Sunday School Lesson twice
attempts to pass the collection plate by mention-
ing the "insufficient funds" with which UN must
struggle, but that how in spite of this "it is doing
a marvelous work." And to make sure the point
is not overlooked, the youth are again told that
we Americans "should work through UN and
appropriate more funds to finance the activities
of its technical experts." Of course nothing is
said about how we as Americans are already
paying over 41% of the costs of operating the UN,
plus many extras such as bond purchases and
special projects.

From this verbose presentation of the UN and
the need for the one worldism of mass man,
we consider the *Methodist Adult Quarterly* of
September 1962 in which were presented five
lessons on the subject of "Christianity and Communism." There is no subtlety in the writer's
approach, for it is stated that the lessons are
designed to make people think "we deceive our-

selves if we visualize Communism in stark black
and white as absolute evil opposed to our absolute good."

Communism is anti-God, anti-Christ; it affirms that man has no soul, and must give his
life to being a slave of the State; it destroys
his initiative, increases his want, spreads his
misery. Where is there good to be found in any
of this? Furthermore, the lesson writer projects
the idea that communism "offers its followers
a remarkably unified, consistent, integrated interpretation of the origin or society and man's
place in it."

Since communism has proved totally inadequate in supplying the needs of society, the lesson writer naturally must try to minimize the
fact, and he does so by asserting the shocking
statement, "At least Communism promises, and
sometimes Communism delivers where democracy — even Christianity — has failed." Churches
whose emphases are abnormally placed upon
the social aspects of the Gospel have failed;
men who would content themselves to newly
clothe the bum but show no concern for a newly
created heart have failed; ministers whose messages have lost the redeeming ring of the New
Birth have failed; but Christianity has never
failed! If a man goes blind he may claim the sun
ceases to shine, but its brillance is unmodified to
hom whose sight remains.

Identifying himself even more completely in
the Socialist camp, the lesson writer asserts
that,

"We withhold understanding and help from underdeveloped
nations which find some socialistic-type of government essential. Certainly in its ideal form, a system which stresses
equality and cooperation should come nearer Christian
principles than one which is frankly based on competition
and the "survival of the fittest."

Why have some underdeveloped nations found a "Socialist type of government essential"? The Socialist structure very simply enhances the power of the despotic and tyrannical rulers and better assists in the absolute control of the people. Anyone who believes socialism "stresses equality and cooperation" and that these values are "nearer Christian principles than one which is frankly based on competition and 'the survival of the fittest,'" simply reveals his ignorance of free enterprise. In competitive capitalism the competition is to see who can improve the quality of the product, or produce it for less cost. The "fittest" who "survive" are those who serve their fellowmen best, who do the most for people and grow and prosper because of it. Naturally, some fail to serve the welfare of the people because of a lack in efficiency or a failure to cut costs; but because of the challenge of free enterprise they turn failure into success in another area and profit by the lesson.

In an apparent effort to hide some of the ugliness of Communism, the quarterly asks its readers to "realize that Iron Curtains face two ways. . ." Should they not rather be reminded that the mass exodus has been from East Berlin, not into it; that multitudes fled Hungary never to return to it; that Cuba is no longer homeland to the thousands who seek escape from it? There have been walls erected to hold out the invader, fences structured to discourage the attacker, ditches furrowed to foil the enemy, but there has never been a predecessor that compares to the Iron Curtain captivity that was plotted for the one purpose of stopping the flight of fettered humanity to freedom.

If the above evidence has not shown the trend toward the left in the church's educational arm, the following quotation taken from the October, 1960 issue of the Methodist *"Motive"* magazine for college youth should clinch it.

"The most obvious comment a visitor must make on the American political scene concerns the Marxist bugbear. For ten years or more Americans have been conditioned to believe that Marxism is the ultimate evil and must be destroyed. . . It is hard to get objective thinking on this subject. Although the task is not easy and although he who endeavors to unmask this myth will be easily misunderstood, yet that task has to be done. . . The ideology of Marxism appears to provide an emotional overtone which is needed to awaken the masses from their centuries of lethargy."

These words would require no alteration to fit comfortably into an editorial of *Pravda* or *Isvestia*. Furthermore, this call to pedantry was forerun by an earlier issue of *"Motive"* that called for a rejection of the need of Christ by the words, "Can one be saved only through Christ? Is not such a claim idolatrous?" and of a solicitation to blasphemy and immorality with the poem,

"Thou shalt not be crude or cave-manish in love-making; and, above all, thou shalt not be guility of chastity."

"Blessed are the broad-minded, for they do not disturb you with their Victorian scruples."

"Blessed are the impure in heart, for they make such enjoyable companions."

"Our Fathers, who art in Madison Avenue . . . give us this day our daily Martini, and forgive us our goofs, even as we try to overlook the goofs of others. And, for heaven's sake, our Lords, lead us into temptation, and deliver us from the Puritans. For thine is the kingdom and the Power and the Glory — if not forever, at least until someone sharper than you comes along.

Amen and amen."

Some of course are not as bold in their blasphemy, but are yet more forward in their advocacy of immorality. Professor Joseph Fletcher of the Episcopal Theological School in Cambridge, Mass., seeks to undermine the Biblical moral standard by expounding such advice as, "even a transient sex liaison, if it has the elements of caring, of tenderness of selfless concern, is better than a mechanical, egocentric exercise of conjugal 'rights' between two uncaring or antagonistic marriage partners." (*Time*, January 21, 1966)

Dr. Fletcher's "situation ethics" blurs values so completely that he can then content himself by sitting in judgment upon what wrong is less harmful than what other wrong, or what evil is more injurious than what other evil. To him there is little if any absolute truth. Every act, good or bad, must be judged within its context. What is immorality to one couple is not immorality to another; the act of adultery in one situation would be an act of innocence in another.

Perhaps it would be more comfortable for Dr. Fletcher's maverick brand of morality if Jesus had not told the woman taken in adultery to "go, and sin no more" (John 8:11). Even though she was caught "in the very act," Dr. Fletcher, before claiming it was "sin," would probably have questioned her first to see how she went about the act, to determine if she had "the elements of caring."

How strangely allied is this to the Communist dogma which affirms the adultery is wrong unless it advances the cause of the State. Immorality, too, is a valuable tool if the State can be served as a result of the act. Both Dr. Fletcher and Communist dogma depend upon the "situation" to determine right and wrong.

Just recently in Chicago's historic First Congregational church, in a service largely attended by the delegates of the United Church of Christ's General Synod, Rev. J. Archie Hargraves conducted a litany on slum life. Portions of that litany, in which the people were asked by Rev. Hargraves to "get loose and loose and more loose," are here given.

Leader: O God, who lives in tenements, who goes to segregated schools, who is beaten in precincts, who is unemployed —

Congregation: Help us to know you.

Leader: O God, who hangs on street corners, who tastes the grace of cheap wine and the sting of the needle —

Congregation: Help us to touch you.

Leader: O God, who is pregnant without husband, who is child without parent, who has no place to play —

Congregation: Help us to know you.

Leader: O God, who can't read or write, who is on welfare, and who is treated like garbage. . .

Congregation: Help us to know you.

Leader: O God, whose name is spic, black nigger, bastard guinea and kike —

Congregation: Help us to know you.

Leader: O God, who is cold in the slums of winter, whose playmates are rats — four-legged one who live with you and two-legged ones who imprison you —

Congregation: Help us to touch you.

Leader: O God, who is white and lives with Mr. Charlie, who is black and lives with Uncle Tom —

Congregation: Help us to see you.

Leader: O God, who smells and has no place to bathe —

Congregation: Help us to be with you.

Leader: O God, who hustles 50 cents for lousy wine, who sells copper and lead to clean his clothes —

Congregation: Help us to touch you.

Where does all this lead? What is the intent of these and a multitude of like actions, assertions, and allegations? It lays, very simply, in the desire to alter the orbit of Christianity, to change the concepts of freedom, to secure Socialism's seizure, or to eleminate free-enterprise's excellence. The shift of the battle may depend on the reaction, acceptance or rejection, of the rank and file of the members of the churches.

Herbert A.
Philbrick

Chapter 7

Another tool

SUBVERTING YOUTH
WITH FOLKSINGING

HERBERT A. PHILBRICK

Herbert A. Philbrick worked nine years with the Communists while counter-spying on them for the FBI. His testimony at the trial of the eleven top U. S. Communists before Judge Harold Medina in 1949 cracked the Communist defense and helped convict them of conspiring to overthrow the U. S. Government.

"Knowing how the Communists operate," Mr. Philbrick said in a recent interview, "as well as the techniques they use to spread their influence through the ranks of American citizenry, I want to warn that anyone, no matter how innocent, can unwittingly become a dupe of the Communists. Quietly, imperceptibly, they infiltrate the most worthy organizations, involving innocent men and women in their schemes."

Unlike a great many Americans, Mr. Philbrick beat the Communists at their own game before being caught in the great conspiracy. In 1940 he discovered they had very quietly taken over the reins of a suburban youth group he headed outside of Boston, Massachusetts. Instead of resigning in the heat of his first anger, he went to the FBI for advice. They suggested he stay in and learn what the Communists were going to do. After making the difficult decision to stay Philbrick let himself apparently be argued over to the Communist way of thinking, joined the Young Communist League in 1942 and two years later, he was invited to join the Party. After taking this fateful step, Philbrick gradually rose in the Party ranks until he was made a member of the Pro-4 group, which masterminded Communist strategy in the area.

As a member of the inner circle, Philbrick for instance saw the Communists trick innocent clergymen into signing petitions, circulate them among other reputable individuals who would add their names on the basis of the previous signers, and then alter the wording of the petitions.

Another tool

SUBVERTING YOUTH
WITH FOLKSINGING

by Herbert A. Philbrick

*It is well known that music can be used to charm
snakes. Not so well known; music can be used
by snakes to charm people.*

During the course of my frequent lecture
tours, come Sundays, I usually drop into a
church; whichever church happens to be closest
to the hotel. In so doing, it has been my pleasure
to attend a number of Lutheran services, and
thus to become acquainted with a number of
Lutheran pastors. I have been most favorably
impressed by the high caliber of the excellent
sermons I have been privileged to hear. I can
report that I have never at any time heard a
single sermon which approached anything that
might be called pro-Communist or anti-
American; indeed, many of the messages were
decidedly and pointedly anti-Communist.

Also, researchers who have probed the matter
of Communist infiltration in the churches have
found that the Lutheran Church has one of the
cleanest records of any of the various denominations. Although I have not queried him specifically as to this matter, I am sure that Dr. J. B.
Mathews, unquestionably the leading expert in
the nation in his field, would confirm that the
list of Lutheran Pastors with records of communist front affiliations is among the smallest

of the various lots.

It is, therefore, with a sense of genuine sadness and dismay that I read of a very foolish and needless controversy among and between my Lutheran friends because a notoriously known, publicly identified member of the Communist apparatus had been engaged as a paid performer for the Walther League International Convention which was held in (July) at Squaw Valley, California. The Walther League is an association of Lutheran young people, with headquarters in the Lutheran Youth Building, 875 North Dearborn Street, Chicago, Ill. It boasts a membership of several thousand of the finest youth of our land.

The resulting — and predictable — uproar has not only produced the old familiar charges and countercharges, but has tended to focus attention upon an area not often discussed in the fight for freedom; that of communist infiltration and subversion in the field of folksinging. Hences, it seems appropriate at this time to deal with a few facts relative to this matter.

Why Folksinging?

At first glance, the folksinging field would appear to be a most unlikely target for communism. After all, folk songs are almost as old as history; they are today a major form of fun, entertainment and amusement; and to the professionals in the entertainment world, a highly lucrative and profitable business. What can be wrong with that?

Unfortunately, the wily Reds see the whole picture in a much different light, for two reasons: music is a powerful medium to reach the emotions of people; and music can be used not merely to entertain, but to convey a message; it is another means of "communication", hence of immediate practical interest to the agit-prop division of the communist network.

And indeed, since the dawn of mankind, music has been part of his "language." Neither can there be any question as to the emotional appeal of music. All of the great religions of the civilized world — the Protestant and Catholic Churches, the Jewish Synagogues — include music as a part of their worship to God. Anyone attending a Billy Graham crusade rally can attest to the powerful emotional impact of the musical section of the program.

The same impact is to be found in the great national anthems of the civilized world. Tuckerman has pointed out that "explain it as we may, a martial strain will urge a man into the front rank of battle sooner than an argument, and a fine anthem excites his devotion more certainly than a logical discourse."

Enter The Communists

How did the Reds get into the act? According to the State of California Senate Fact-finding Committee, which conducted an extensive investigation in the field, the two major mediums have been "People's Songs, Inc.," and "People's Artists". Their report, published in 1951, said: (in part):

"People's Songs, Inc. was incorporated on January 31, 1946, in New York City . . . it has injected itself into Communist fronts, and Communist Schools, and left-wing trade union and political activity.

"Advertisements and press notices for its activities are to be found in the *Daily Worker*, *New Masses*, *The Worker*, *Chicago Star*, *Michigan Herald*, *People's Daily World*, and *Salute*.

"So important have the songs produced by

People's Songs, Inc., become in Red ranks that the Communist school in Hollywood (People's Educational Center, later absorbed by the Communist California Labor School in San Francisco) and the Jefferson School in New York have inaugurated classes in the science of agitational song writing. They are taught by leaders of People's Songs, Inc.

"People's Artists is also an affiliate of People's Songs, and it has offices in with the latter group. It supplies special talent to organizations for the purpose of promoting 'people's songs' shows, and entertainment. People's Artists also supplies the entertainment for Communist Party gatherings. It took charge of the entertainment at a party meeting which was held in New York.

"The Committee finds that People's Songs is a vital Communist Front . . . which has spawned a horde of lesser fronts in the field of music, stage, entertainment, choral singing, folk dancing, recording, radio transcriptions and similar fields.

"It especially is important to Communist proselytizing and propaganda work because of its emphasis on appeal to youth and because of its organization and technique to provide entertainment for organizations and groups as a smooth opening wedge for Marxist-Leninist-Stalinist propaganda."

Enter Pete Seeger

When it came to setting up the program for the Walther League Convention in Chicago, for some strange reason, out of the literally hundreds of highly talented performers in the folksinging field, the one man selected by the adult leaders of the Lutheran youth organization was none

other than Pete Seeger, whose cooperation and
support for communist causes has received extensive coverage in the Annual Reports of the
House Committee on Un-American Activities
(Page 124, 1959 Report; pages 51 and 117, 1960
Report; and page 43, 1961 Report) as well as in
other official reports.

Although the President of the Missouri Synod,
Dr. Oliver R. Harms, advised against following
through with the convention program plans, and
was upheld in his suggestion by the Vice Presidents and a majority of the District Presidents,
the militant minority leaders at the Chicago
Walther League headquarters have chosen to
retain Mr. Seeger on the program.

Even worse, however, is that they published
an enormous amount of false statements and allegations in defense of Mr. Seeger, and have
further bitterly attacked and defamed their own
Lutheran pastors who objected to the employment of the identified Communist entertainer.

As could easily have been predicted, the powerful *Christian Century* magazine also took
the pro-communist side of the controversy, as it
almost always does, and launched a bitter attack
against Lutheran ministers and leaders. Those
Lutherans who objected to the appearance of
Seeger were smeared by the *Christian Century* as "hatemakers," "rightists", "right wing
agitators", and as "orthodoxists" (the last term
apparently another dirty word in the *Christian
Century* dictionary).

The Christian Century has followed a
long-standing policy of devoting a great deal
more attention to attacking members of the
Protestant Church than it ever seems to be able
to direct against the Communists. If they criticize the Communists — which is seldom — it

is always in the mildest terms; but when it comes to criticism of ministers of the Gospel, they do not hesitate to indulge in name calling and smears, and in so doing to use caustic and vehement language.

Tragically, the pro-Seeger minority in the Walther League adopted the same tactics, and in so doing have carried out a campaign of vilification against members of their own Church far more extensive than anything I can recall in the Communist press. It is for sure that the ten thousand Communists in this country watched this spectacle with smug satisfaction.

Bunkum

In addition, the defenders of the Seeger appearance have, in support of their position, used many arguments which have done nothing except to expose their abysmal ignorance about communism and the laws having to do with the Communist conspiracy, thus giving support to the adage, "It is better to remain silent and let people think you are a fool, rather than open your mouth and prove it."

Here are some samples, for their published statements:

BUNK: "Why disturb the church over the appearance of a folksinger?"

FACT: Hundreds of prominent Lutherans have protested, not the appearance of a folksinger, but the paid employment of a publicly identified Communist. If the adult officials of the Walther League are unable to discern the difference between the two, they should be relieved from positions of responsibility and be given employment more in keeping with their limited mental capabilities.

BUNK: "Thorough investigation does not substatiate accusations that Mr. Seeger is a Communist or a Communist sympathizer".

FACT: So far as I can discover, no other entertainer in America has been linked with more Communist and Communist front organizations, in the past 15 years, either as a speaker, member, official, teacher, participant or performer, than has Pete Seeger. Indeed, his record is one of the longest of any person, in any profession, in the entire United States. The Church League of America compiled a list of only the publicly announced affiliations and found that they filled twenty-four printed pages.

As for membership: Herb Romerstein, in his book, *"Communism and Your Child"*, points out that Mr. Seeger has been identified as a member of the Communist Party by a number of sources including the Communist *"Daily Worker"* of May 4, 1949, which identified Seeger as a member of the Music Section of the Cultural Division of the Communist Party.

BUNK: (a) "Mr. Seeger has been charged with being a Communist. (b) He declined before a Congressional Committee to answer the charges. (c) He has not been convicted in a court of law."

FACT: (a) As we have already pointed out, Seeger was not merely "charged" or "accused to be", a Communist; he was identified as a member, by the Communist Party's official newspaper, as well as by others. (b) Because he obviously possessed information about the activities of the Communist Party, he was called before the House investigating committee and given an opportunity to present, in sworn testimony, such information which would aid Congress in any necessary remedial legislation. Seeger contemptuously refused to reveal any of the factual data he was known to possess.

(c) Convicted of what Being a Communist? Seeger has never been charged with being a Communist in any court of law, for the simple reason
that it is not illegal to be a Communist in the
United States; hence, no person has ever been so
convicted. Such a statement is a ludicrous as to
allege that since no one has ever been convicted
of being Lutheran, there are no Lutherans in the
United States.

BUNK: "He (Seeger) was cited for contempt
but was cleared by a higher court of law."

FACT: Seeger was not merely "cited" but was
indicted and tried before a Jury, and was found
guilty of contempt and sentenced by the Court to
one year in prison. Later, on appeal, the conviction was reversed on the legal technicality
that the indictment was faultily drawn. In no way
does this mean that he was "cleared".

Such are some of the arguments; many more,
equally inaccurate and untrue, have been used in
a stubborn attempt by the Walther League officials to defend an untenable policy. Indeed, these
attempts have done more to damage the prestige
and honor of the Walther League far more than
the original invitation itself, and have only served
to degrade the organization in the eyes of
thoughtful people.

The Messages

A study of the lyrics in the so called "folk
songs" enjoyed by the Communist would make a
book in itself. Many of them are in the guise of
"humor"; but a very sick kind of humor; snide,
bitter denunciation of all things based upon love
of country or love for God. Many of the slanted
lyrics are in the form of protest; and, or course,
they protest all things that normal people are

against; war; the atom bomb; hunger; poverty; slums; discrimination. Crime, they are not against; indeed, the criminal, the jail bird or the thief is frequently glorified. Also glorified, of course, are "the peepul" . . . but not all people; only the "working class peepul". The "little man" is pictured as the hopeless, hapless pawn of the capitalist system; he is a victim of the existing social order; and the only way out (naturally) is for a socialist government to come to his rescue, to provide for his wants and needs, and propel him into a bright new world without war, without poverty, without greed — truly, a paradise on earth, equalled only by the Soviet Union.

One of the so-called folk songs, currently very popular in Communist circles, is called "Cod Liver Oil", (*)

The verses begin, "I'm a might poor man with a worrisome life; ten years I've been wedded to a sickly wife". The poor wife, it develops, is in such bad shape that all she does is "nothing all day but sit down and cry and a-wishin to God that she would die".

Ah! But this is not just a "blues" song. It has a message. The answer to this horrible state of affairs, it turns out, is Medicare; "It's government sponsored and they pay the bill".

Of course, the song does not point out that the government can't pay for anything unless it takes the money away from the people first; or, if the original song did contain such a verse, somebody should tell the composer that the Communists aren't singing that part.

At a recent Communist sponsored meeting held in New York, one of the songs contained the lines, "If you want progress, then join with CORE; it's been a long time since the civil war;" and, "Nothing could be finer, than to crash an all-white diner, and land up in the jail on time". (*)

Still another, now going the rounds in Communist bookstores, is called "The Draft Dodger Rag" (*). It begins with the lines, "I'm just a typical American boy from a typical American town; I believe in God and Senator Dodd and in keeping old Castro down".

As the verses go on, however, it turns out that the alleged typical American boy has a yellow streak a yard wide and the spine of a jellyfish. It contains the message: "But one thing, Sarge, you gotta see; that someone's gotta go over there, and that someone isn't me; if you ever get a war without blood and gore, well, I'll be the first to go".

The Communists are very selective in their "humorous" songs. Many people will recall "The Preacher and the Bear" as a song which was funny, not foul; it was laughable, but not sacrilegious. But those in Party favor, such as "Plastic Jesus" (*) and "On God's Side" (*) are sarcastic and bitter. They are not "funny" or "humorous"; they are simply hateful.

To Summarize

It would be utterly insane to allege that modern folk singing is one great big Communist plot; or that folk singing is evil, or subversive; or that "all" folk singers are secret Communists, hiding behind the frets of their guitars. I would hope (but do not expect) that witch-hunters Forster, Epstein, Janson, Eismann and company will have the decency not to distort the meaning and intent of this report into "an attack against folk singing". Let the record show that I have not made such an attack, either by word, implication or innuendo.

At the same time, I believe that it is vitally important for people to know that members of the Communist criminal conspiracy have, beyond any shadow of doubt, endeavored to infiltrate, manipulate and use the field of folk singing, in order to serve the cause of communism, by means of clever and vicious attacks against the cause of freedom, liberty, justice and independence as exemplified by the United States of America, the last hope of the down-trodden and oppressed peoples of the world today.

If any lessons are to be learned from the Lutheran controversy, it is to point up the great need for accurate information as to the machinations and methods, as well as the aims and goals, of the Communist conspiracy in this country. I am sure that if the leaders of the Walther League had been aware of these facts, the idiotic plans for their July program would never have been made.

(*) Disclaimer: I have no knowledge of the origin of this, or the other songs mentioned; nor do I have any information as to their authors, composers; nor do I allege that they are Communist or pro-Communist. The fact that the Communists may like a particular lyric does not constitute evidence that the author or composer is a Communist. At the same time, it would seem reasonable to suggest that songwriters should take pains NOT to write lyrics that can be used against us.

G. Aiken
Taylor

Chapter 8

Power Blocs, Power Politics and

THE NATIONAL COUNCIL
OF CHURCHES

G. AIKEN TAYLOR

G. Aiken Taylor was born in Recife, Brazil, the son of George W. Taylor and Julia Pratt Taylor, Presbyterian Missionaries. At the age of fifteen he returned to this country to complete his education, graduating from the Presbyterian College of South Carolina with the A. B. degree in 1940. After teaching in the public schools of South Carolina for a year, he entered the Army and throughout more than three years with the 36th (Texas) Infantry Division, he rose to the rank of Captain, commanding a heavy weapons company in the 142nd Infantry. He participated in five major campaigns, was wounded once and decorated twice.

After the war, he entered the Columbia Theological Seminary of Decatur, Georgia, graduating with the B. D. degree, magna cum laude, in 1948. Later, he was awarded the Ph.D., degree by Duke University for work done on *John Calvin, The Teacher,* a study of Religious Education in Calvin's Geneva.

Dr. Taylor has served as pastor of Presbyterian churches in Smyrna, Ga., Burlington, N. C. and Alexandria, La. He is now the editor of *The Presbyterian Journal,* with offices in Asheville, N. C. He is the author of two books, *A Sober Faith,* now in its third printing, and *St. Luke's Life Of Jesus.*

He is married to the former Blanche Williams of Chattanooga, Tenn., and they have four children, George, Jane, Hugh and Julia.

Power Blocs, Power Politics and

THE NATIONAL COUNCIL
OF CHURCHES

by G. Aiken Taylor

The average church member is understandably troubled whenever he sees or hears another defense of the National Council of Churches against alleged "slanderous attacks bred in ignorance and fed on misinformation." There is reason to believe the defense itself is bred in ignorance and fed on misinformation!

Official defenses of the NCC continue to appear in the Church press. Invariably, they stress the value of the great work which the Churches are doing through the NCC — rejecting the criticisms by pointing to the cooperative accomplishments of the agencies of the Council: service to migrants, ministry in national parks, relief and rehabilitation of refugees, literacy programs, and so on.

Then the defenders usually repeat the denial that the NCC is trying to become a "super-Church" and dogmatically assert that the NCC is not a "pro-this" or "against-that" organization. Somewhere in the defense almost always a statement appears to this effect: "When the Council makes its views known on issues of Christian concern, it is the appointed leaders from the member denominations who do the speaking and who issue the considered statements."

HALF OF THE TRUTH

Such defenses of the National Council of Churches are only half of the truth; they do not come to grips with the real criticisms at all. Few people criticize the NCC's service to migrants, or the relief and rehabilitation programs — the work that the Churches do together in the Council. And we know but few who base the greater part of their objections to the Council on its habit of speaking out on legitimate "issues of Christian concern."

The Council has generated criticism by activities which are seldom mentioned in those spirited defenses one sees and hears, and much of it is directed at what the Council itself says and does which is not the saying and the doing of those "appointed leaders of member denominations."

It is against the multitude of ways that the Council's divisions and departments, executives and secretaries, staff members and "experts" — by direct and indirect means — seek to mould and influence, guide and direct, and *control* the member Churches; as well as the direction taken in politics, education and economics, that the criticisms of the Council are mounting.

Most of the ways in which the NCC exerts its influence upon the Churches and upon the country are *outside* the official processes whereby "appointed leaders of member denominations" gather for joint action. Acting on their own initiative (and presumably "speaking only for themselves") these officials, occupying offices at 475 Riverside Drive, New York, plan the programs, pull the strings and issue the directives that ultimately affect the lives of millions of people.

Orders go out — and the teen-age young

people at Ann Arbor, Michigan, are treated to a raucous play, "For Heaven's Sake," which establishes a new worship "form" for the Protestant community.

Bulletins go out — and in due time state governments have appointed official commissions to study problems of unemployment, welfare, housing, or what have you.

Directives go out — and in the end legislation has been introduced in the United States Congress to change our government's policies on immigration, migratory labor, loyalty oaths, and the like. In 1965, some of the amendments to the Administration's Aid to Education bill were known on Capitol Hill as "Flemming Amendments," after the NCC official, Dr. Arthur Flemming, most responsible for getting them in.

Who did more to keep alive the "issue" of the film depicting the 1960 student riots in San Francisco, "Operation Abolition;" and to stress alleged opposition of the Churches to the House Committee on Un-American Activities? For months no other subjects received a fraction of the editorial attention that the NCC devoted to these. Almost every issue of *Religious Newsweekly* and of *News* (NCC Bulletins) reported to editors across the country the names of churchmen and church organizations falling into line with appropriate resolutions. No bulletins reported the possibility that there might be another side to the story. For months every issue of *Interchurch News* (NCC monthly paper) featured editorials and stories slanted to convey the impression of a monstrous danger embodied in anti-Communist groups and congressional investigating committees. Hardly a state or local council of churches failed to fall into line with resolutions of their own. And denominational conventions and assemblies followed suit.

The truth of the matter: the National Council of Churches' professional staff *does* act independently of the member Churches. The council *is* a "pro-this" and "against-that," organization. It already behaves as the headquarters of a super-Church — a sort of Protestant equivalent of the Vatican. In its areas of greatest influence it is — in our opinion — a distinct menace to the autonomy and integrity of its own member Churches.

EXAMPLES OF INFLUENCE

Here is a bulletin dated December, 1959, in which the Department of Religious Liberty of the NCC appealed to the churches and everybody else to write letters of protest against the imprisonment of Willard Uphaus, New Hampshire layman then serving a jail sentence for refusing to give the Attorney General a list of "guests" at his summer camp for "World Fellowship." In that same issue the Department also urged everybody to write the White House on behalf of Morton Sobell, convicted spy in the famous case of Klaus Fuchs, Harry Gold, David Greenglass, Julius Rosenberg, *et al.*

Was this communication issued by the "appointed leaders of the member denominations"? It was not. Nor was it an action of those member denominations and their representatives "working together." It was the brain child of a secretary in the Department of Religious Liberty, sent out on his own authority, not as a directive nor as an official communique, *but with the same effect*.

A landslide of correspondence presumably followed the appearance of this bulletin. Resolutions were adopted by local congregations and city and state councils of churches. Pressure was brought to bear upon the Attorney General of New Hampshire and upon the White House. And all on account of an *independent* action by a department of the NCC speaking only for itself.

This example serves to show how the NCC exerts the greater part of its influence upon the churches; by "messages" on every conceivable subject under the sun from race relations to automation in industry; by pamphlets and tracts and study material and text books and articles; in the opinions of "experts" and "consultants" and "advisers" — executives, secretaries, staff members. In very *few* cases do the member denominations themselves have anything to say about the avalanche of material by which their boards, agencies and ordinary members derive their opinions, establish their policies, prepare their educational literature.

Missions policies, educational procedures, worship patterns, political action — all are influenced and conditioned by this vast headquarters of the Churches which manages to manipulate the Protestant bodies of America while preserving an image of "cooperative action" on the part of "all the Churches working together."

INFLUENCING JOINT ACTION

Even when the action taken is indeed the concerted action of the representatives of the Churches in a study conference or a consultation, the NCC manages to steer the deliberations and influence the outcome of the meeting.

Anyone familiar with the deliberative processes of large assemblies knows how much is prepared in advance and how little is actually done on the floor of the assembly. The NCC leaders are past masters at this sort of thing. Speakers carefully selected by those who plan

and organize the meeting, lay the groundwork in
their addresses for the "resolutions" and "messages" to follow. Draft copies of the resolutions
and messages are circulated with the enthusiastic
endorsement of officials and "experts." When the
resolutions and messages come to the floor of
the assembly for adoption, minor points of dis-
agreement are quickly ironed out. And when the
vote is taken it usually turns out to be a "unan-
imous" action.

This is quite likely the way it went in that
famous Fifth World Order Study Conference in
which the representatives of the Churches voted
to recommend the admission of Red China to
the United Nations. The salient features of the
"message" were determined by executives of the
NCC (or "experts" selected by the staff) in the
offices of the NCC. In the preliminary committee
meetings the opposition which appeared to the
controversial sections of the document was
smoothly put down. In the assembly itself the
final "message" passed without a dissenting vote
(although we know delegates who did not concur
in all of the recommendations). And it is quite
possible that some of the delegates did not
really know what they had voted for until the
storm broke in the newspapers.

In other words, it was 475 Riverside Drive,
New York, which acted in Cleveland, Ohio, in the
Fifth World Order Study Conference, not the
thirty-odd member denominations represented
among the participants.

SPEAKING TO THE CHURCHES

The principal claim of the NCC — that it is a
body speaking *to* the Churches rather than *for* the
Churches — constitutes the ground for the severest complaints against the NCC.

Out of those New York offices pours a veritable flood of opinion-making materials, all of it designed to influence the thinking of Christian people and to influence the actions of Christian Churches. *Most* of it is not "official" in the sense of being the voice of some three dozen denominations speaking. *Most* of it is not even "official" in the sense of being the considered opinion of the representatives of the denominations. *Most* of it is only the voice of executives and staff members and "experts" selected by them, speaking *to* the Churches.

Here is a Labor Sunday Message — drafted by staff members of the NCC and sent out to be read in thousands of pulpits across the land. And here is a Race Relations Sunday message — drafted by staff members of the NCC and sent out to be read in thousands of pulpits across the land. Here are articles on migrants, on religious liberty, on Church and State problems, on the immigration laws of the United States, on Right-to-Work laws, on medical care for the aged under Social Security, on the rights of conscientious objectors.

Here are study books for the denominations to use in their own programs; and films; and "authoritative" text books on everything from camping to economics; and worship materials to be used on special occasions such as the World Day of Prayer.

The denominations have very little to do with the preparation of most of this material; nor do they edit it before it goes out. Their representatives may offer suggestions (as Presbyterian U. S. representatives offered suggestions for improving *Servants of God in People's China,* a World Missions study book for 1963) but the NCC is not bound to take them (as it didn't in the case of *Servants of God in People's China*).

Are the denominations bound to use the material? No, and when it is especially bad a sensitive denomination may leave a particular study
book off its list (as the Presbyterian Church,
U.S., finally left *Servants of God in People's
China* off its list although leaders of the Church's
Department of Campus Christian Life recommended it). Are the denominations compelled to
adopt the teachings enunciated in the material?
No. Then how can it be said that the NCC is
dominating the denominations? Well how better
dominate the thinking of people than by dictating
what they read and hear?

Take another example: Not long ago the Labor
Sunday message was on the danger of *automation* in industry; and about how the Churches
should be interested in doing something about
the evils of automation. That message was drafted
in the offices of the NCC and sent out (as usual)
to be read in thousands of pulpits, over radio,
over TV; and printed in virtually all Church
papers and magazines. Was it a binding pronouncement of the NCC? No. But it had the same
effect. Churches passed resolutions on automation. City and state councils of churches passed
resolutions on automation. More recently state
governments have appointed committees *headed
by clergymen* to study the evils of automation.
Bills have been considered for introduction into
Congress. And why? Because all of the Churches
working together said something? No. Because
the Interchurch Center said something.

Take another example: A couple of years ago
an international conference on problems of immigration was held in Switzerland. Before that
conference convened the National Council of
Churches summoned its own conference on im-

migration. The representatives of the Churches
dutifully came together. As is the case in all
such study conferences, they first heard carefully selected speakers pointing out the "flaws"
in U. S. immigration policies. Then they were
offered a document critical of those policies to
consider. How had the document been drafted?
Under the auspices of the NCC, of course. When
the final draft was approved by the conference,
it went to the international meeting as an expression of the opinion of the American Churches.
The upshot? Resolutions in churches and councils of churches on the "unfair immigration policies of the United States." Most important: resolutions were introduced into Congress designed
to change the immigration policies of the United
States — and in 1965, a new immigration bill was
adopted by the Congress. Where did it all start?
There's no telling where the original idea came
from to involve the Churches in the business of
immigration, but that idea was translated into
action in the offices of the NCC.

One of the severest indictments against the
NCC's political meddling could be leveled on the
basis of what it did to help kill Public Law 78,
which formerly permitted Mexican (and other)
labor to help harvest crops in the South and
Southwest. One of the first pronouncements ever
adopted by the NCC after it was organized was on
"The Concern of the Churches for Agricultural
Migratory Labor" (1951). In 1960 the NCC began
campaigning against Public Law 78 with articles
written by staff members and published by its
Office on The Migrant Ministry. By 1963 religious
groups were beseiging Congress with petitions
to terminate Public Law 78 and the NCC's lobby
office in Washington was mailing out bulletins
reporting the contest. In December, 1964, the

law died.

Political action has been given a high priority by NCC programmers. During 1965, for instance, the NCC:

— Issued a "Call to Action," summoning all churchmen to pressure their congressmen into unseating Mississippi's five incumbent members of the House of Representatives.

— Testified before the Congress against so-called Right-to-Work laws.

— Opposed any constitutional amendment which would allow states to re-apportion one of their upper chambers on any basis other than "one man one vote."

— Demanded changes in U. S. immigration policies.

— Supported the "civil rights" bill, the "poverty" bill, the "medicare" bill and others.

— Criticized America's foreign policy in places such as the Dominican Republic and Viet Nam.

There's the so-called Delta Project of the NCC which originally was to have been an aid program benefitting a designated area in the state of Mississippi. Like many other NCC ventures, the Delta Project has been expanded beyond its original boundaries and has become involved in political and economic action not even remotely related to its alleged religious interest. On the basis of what the NCC calls its "mandate" in Mississippi, the council has in effect preempted many of the functions of local government. It has entered the field of public works, adding to its project ventures into low-rent housing, community development programs, and even loans to small businesses by the federal government.

A MENACE TO THE CHURCHES

It is for activities such as these that we believe the National Council of Churches to be a menace to its own constituency. It is *not* primarily — or even to any considerable extent — a spiritual organization. It is *not* primarily an organization through which the Churches work together. Its greatest influence is *not* exerted by the representatives of the denominations meeting together. It is in effect a closely knit group of executives and other churchmen running the affairs of the Churches by direct and indirect means — looking toward the day when there will be one super-Church in America with a single headquarters.

It is not even sensitive to the wishes of its constituency. When an official communication comes up from some denomination, as from the 1964 General Assembly of the Presbyterian Church U.S., the communication may be filed without even being read to the General Board.

It is patently untrue that the NCC does not seek to become a super-Church. This is possibly true of the vast majority of its constituents, but they have very little to do with determining their own plans and programs these days.

In the future we can expect the NCC to continue to tighten its control over the programs and the planning of the denominations. Its youth meetings will continue to feature off-beat dramas and shocking films. Its denominations will continue to bring their Christian Education curricula closer and closer together by coordinating them under the authority of text books prepared by NCC "experts." (At this moment a dozen denominations are cooperating in the production of new educational literature under the benevolent oversight of the National Council of Churches.)

It will more and more be recognized as the home "board" for all the foreign mission work of its denominations. It will more and more plan the location of local congregations as new churches are established "cooperatively" by home missions boards "working together." Higher education and seminary education in America will more and more conform to patterns established within its offices or by its consultants. One of these days military chaplains and chaplains for the House and the Senate may well be appointed by the appropriate department of the NCC — even as it has now begun to appoint overseas pastors of churches serving American personnel in various centers around the world.

The direction of movement is mostly socialistic and hostile to the historic interpretation of the Gospel theologically, politically, economically and ecclesiastically. There is one super-Church aborning for the constituent denominations blindly following the NCC. And the signs are that it will bear little resemblance to the New Testament Church when it grows up.

James
DeForest
Murch

Chapter 9

Reds and

THE WORLD COUNCIL
OF CHURCHES

JAMES DEFOREST MURCH

James DeForest Murch, Washington, D. C., is an ordained minister of the Christian Church (Disciples of Christ). He has especially served in the field of religious journalism having been managing editor of the Standard Publishing Company, manager and editor of *United Evangelical Action* (official organ of the National Association of Evangelicals), and managing editor of *Christianity Today.*

He is the author of over 20 books, among which are *Christian Education and the Local Church, Christians Only* (a history of the Christian Churches and Churches of Christ), *Cooperation without Compromise* (a history of the National Association of Evangelicals), *Teach Me to Pray, God Still Lives, Church-State Relations: the American Way, and Teach or Perish.*

A strong believer in backing up his beliefs by aggressive Christian action he has served in many capacities in such national organizations as the International Society of Christian Endeavor, the National Sunday School Association (President), National Religious Broadcasters (President), National Evangelical Press Association (President), National Association of Christian Schools, North American Christian Convention, International Convention of Disciples of Christ, National Association of Evangelicals, and the National Society Sons of the American Revolution.

Dr. Murch has received honorary doctorates from Northwest Christian College (D. D.) and Milligan College (Litt. D.). His Alma Mater, Ohio University, recently gave him its Distinguished Service Award for attainments in the field of religion. He is a fellow of the International Institute of Arts and Letters and holds membership is a number of honorary fraternities and societies. He has for many years been listed in *Who's Who in America.*

Reds and

THE WORLD COUNCIL
OF CHURCHES

by James DeForest Murch

In an Assembly of 352 delegates representing 135 denominational bodies, the World Council of Churches was officially founded in Amsterdam in 1948. The Council now has 200 churches in its membership with a constituency of approximately 315 million in all parts of the world. It is truly "a mighty army" with ever increasing power. It includes millions who are ignorant of its nature, its functions, and its purposes, but its leadership has a firm grip on its machinery and is moving toward the development of a worldwide ecclesiastical power comparable to that of the Roman Catholic Church.

As early as Amsterdam the red hand of international communism was seen both in the Commission of the Churches on International Affairs and the Council itself. Dr. Joseph Hromadka, official representative of the Evangelical Church of the Czech Brethren, an admitted Communist, openly attacked Western culture which, he asserted, would eventually disappear before the victorious march of Red communism. He said the West was already in ruins and utterly impotent either to preserve itself or to offer successful opposition to the virile upsurge of the proletariat. He expressed agreement with those dogmatic Marxists who believe in the inevitable result of the dialectical process whereby a class-

less society will be built on the ruins of bour-
geois capitalism, no matter who opposes or sup-
ports it. Hromadka held that communism is
essentially a constructive movement growing out
of the Christian tradition and will ultimately be
accepted by all nations. He was wined and dined
by American liberals at Amsterdam, many of
whom had been introduced to him when he was a
member of the faculty of Princeton Theological
Seminary. There were other communists at Amsterdam, notably Dr. C. T. Chao of Red China,
who was elected one of the presidents of the
World Council in the concluding plenary sessions.

Since Amsterdam the advocates of communist,
capitalist, and socialist views in the World Council have been in a continuous clash concerning
the phraseology of its pronouncements on the
world social order. The "voice of God" which is
claimed for its socio-political doctrines has
shifted from one side of the spectrum to the
other, as though God is having difficulty in making up His mind as to whose side He is on. No
declaration has satisfied every body, and the
ecumenical ardor of some has been cooled by
distasteful decisions, usually to the left of center.

At Evanston (1954), where the final, legal decisions were made which gave the Council permanent form, the main social concerns of the
Assembly found expression in a report on "A
Responsible Society in a World Perspective". As
usual, liberal elements were in control of the
study groups and the drafting committees. Representatives from Iron Curtain churches were
much in evidence. Among them were Dr. Hromadka (to whom reference has already been made),
General Bishop Jan Chabada of the Evangelical
Church in Slovakia, Bishop Emerich Varga of the
Reformed Christian Church in Hungary, Bishops

Albert Bereczky, John Peter and Laszlo Pap of the Reformed Church in Hungary, and Bishops Niklot Beste and Gottfried Noth of the Lutheran Church in the Soviet Zone of East Germany, together with a whole retinue of communist assistants. These men were quite vocal in their communistic socialistic views, tempered possibly by the fact that they were on American soil and under considerable criticism by the press. The resultant Council pronouncement stressed the necessity for a "responsible society" (intimating that the current society was not responsible), a "planned economy", an "equitable distribution of wealth", and "peaceful coexistence with communism". So favorable was the dubious phraseology of the report to communism, that the Red delegates highly praised it and indicated that they expected to use it to teach communism in their churches. The communist *Daily Worker* approved the report in a news story headed "Churchmen Urge End of East-West Tension".

It is only fair to say that there is much to commend in some Council studies and reports. They have taken a strong stand for basic human rights, responsibility of governments to God and to the people for social justice and public order, religious freedom, improvement of living conditions, and social opportunities for the underprivileged, assistance to refugees, orphans, sick and aging. The Christian churches must, of course, make clear that they are unequivocally on the side of righteous principle in personal and societal affairs even to the point of open break with those who advocate or practice oppression and injustice in any form. But the Council at Evanston with all its expressions of deep concern in these areas, had little or no criticism of world communism's atheistic, totalitarian enslavement of a third of mankind.

It may be well at this point to consider in some depth both the World Council's social and political views as evidenced in the actions and pronouncements.

It may be said with some degree of accuracy that the Council's chief concern (beyond ecumenicity) is socio-political. Its meetings are filled with discussions about communism, socialism and capitalism on the one hand and the United Nations, peaceful coexistence and atomic warfare on the other. When the theme, "Christ the Hope of the World", with all the theological implications, was chosen for the Evanston Assembly, the editor of the left-wing *Christian Century,* said Evanston could be remembered "as the place where the World Council discovered how quickly the impulse to Christian unity in action could be sidetracked and reduced to impotence" by an emphasis on theology. Supporting the old "liberal" contention that "doctrine divides and social action unites," he went on to say, "Evanston made the surprising disclosure that the social action which the church has been so nervous about lately, stepped forward confidently to save the day. And the theology which has recently been so sure of itself, got absolutely nowhere at all." Boldly the editor of the *Century* contended that the social order should be the chief concern of the WCC.

And while we are quoting the *Century* we might add its bitter note concerning those whose prime concern is doctrine: "If four more assemblies handle theological and dogmatic themes as badly as this one did, the outlook is not encouraging. Give the World Council about four more such theological or dogmatic main themes — say, the nature of Biblical authority in 1960, the nature

of the church in 1966, the nature of salvation in
1972, and the creedal nature of the Council's
own being in 1978 — and if the world itself hasn't
blown up by that time, the Council almost certainly will." Since Evanston the *Century* has had
little to complain about.

The Council's antagonism to capitalism has
been well stated by Dr. John C. Bennett and his
liberal conferees at Amsterdam: "(1) Capitalism
tends to subordinate what should be the primary
task of any economy — the meeting of human
needs — to the economic advantages of those
who have most power over its institutions. (2) It
tends to produce serious inequalities. (3) It has
developed a practical form of materialism in
Western nations in spite of their Christian background, for it has placed the greatest emphasis
upon success in making money. (4) It has also
kept the people of capitalist countries subject to
a kind of fate which has taken the form of such
social catastrophes as mass unemployment."

In the same report ("The Church and Disorder
in Society") these kind words were spoken for
communism: "Christians should ask why communism in its modern totalitarian form makes
so strong an appeal to great masses of people in
many parts of the world. They should recognize
the work of God in the revolt of multitudes
against injustice that gives communism much of
its strength. They should seek to recapture for
the church the original Christian solidarity with
the world's distressed people . . . Christians should
realize that for many, especially for many young
men and women, communism seems to stand for
a vision of human equality and universal brotherhood for which they were prepared by Christian
influences."

While seeking the accommodation necessary to

keep both capitalist and communist elements
active in the Council affairs there is always an
undercurrent of opposition to capitalism and
friendliness to communism. Council leaders warn
against "the temptation to succumb to anti-communist hysteria and the danger of a self-righteous
assurance concerning the political and social
systems of the West." When they warn against
"identifying Christianity with the 'prevailing political and economic systems'", they are saying
that American capitalism and American free
enterprise and American democracy are un-
Christian and ought to be replaced by another
system. They have much to say about a "responsible society" which they define as something other than the social order we now have.
In plain terms, the "liberals" are still in position
to institute some form of planned economy for
the purpose of achieving what they conceive to
be a more equable distribution of wealth (often
referred to as "social justice"). They quote
Amsterdam, Evanston, and New Delhi when they
carry their propaganda into the churches where
study groups have been set up by the World and
National Councils of Churches. Giving "book,
chapter and verse" from these Reports they can
advocate governmental planning and government
control, urge the churches to gain political power
and then, by state coercion, impose a welfare
state on the people whether they want it or not.
This means a degree of socialism. How much
they want is not yet apparent, but that they are
enemies of capitalism and democracy as America has known these institutions for a couple
hundred years is beyond question.

Among the specific commitments of the Council, in the reports and papers issued from Geneva,
we find advocacy of redistribution of population,

birth control, family planning, newly-evolving forms of morality, protection of arbitrary arrest, more lenient parole of criminals, insurance against unemployment, compulsory labor union membership, capitalistic reforms which will reduce employers to the status of "servants of freedom and welfare", planned economy, equitable distribution of wealth, the increase of control by national and international government over employers, farmers and professional groups, international economic controls, and outlawry of war. A complete list of leftwing socio-political doctrines emanating from Geneva would fill a volume. While releases to the press go out on World Council news sheets and get headlines which attribute these doctrines to the Council, Geneva frequently denies their official character by the subterfuge that they represent only the views of Commissions, committees or other groups. It is passing strange that only leftist propaganda is contained in these pronouncements whatever their nature may be.

The United Nations is treated with reverential awe as an organization fully in harmony with the principles of God's moral government. The UN undoubtedly has its proper uses, but this characterization we deny. The Moslems, Hindus, Confucians, Roman Catholics and infidels far outnumber the Protestant representatives in all UN bodies and what little moral or religious atmosphere the UN has is far removed from New Testament Christianity. Of course God was not invoked when the UN was formed and its whole structure, principle and procedure are without benefit of religion. Politically, the UN is foreign to the Christian way of life. Its Asiatic and South American representatives are accustomed to arbitrary government control. Its European dele-

gates are predominantly Socialist or Communist.
They have never known freedom as it exists in
the Christian states. These men assume that
nothing can be accomplished save through government regulations and regimentation. Yet the
Council fully endorses the UN.

The World Council through its accredited agencies is deeply involved in world politics and
seeks all "proper liaison" between the churches
and the states.

According to Dr. O. Frederick Nolde, the
Council's semi-political structure, which has
progressively developed "involves contacts on
the one hand with representative Christian leaders around the world and on the other hand with
intergovernmental and other official organs where
policies are shaped and decisions made." The
men and women charged with this responsibility
have specialized competence and experience in
international affairs, come from twenty-seven
countries. Active national commissions cooperate
with Geneva, their impact on their own governments varying in accordance with specific national circumstances. Additional contacts with
the churches are maintained through special
correspondents. Thus lines run out from the
Council to many parts of the world for prompt
consultation or for transmission of information.
By this means it seeks to keep informed about
varying Christian points of view sometimes involving sharp differences, and to deduce where
possible a common line of action. Since complete
unanimity on grave controversial issues is often
not attainable, representation, if it is to be made
at all, must be made to reflect such views as are
held by a large majority.

In its contact with intergovernmental bodies
Geneva maintains its freedom to suggest, com-

mand, or criticize in accordance with the policies laid down by its commissions and the parent bodies. It has consultative status with the United Nations Economic and Social Council, with UNESCO, with the Food and Agricultural Organization, and working relations with numerous other organs. Because the Council's representatives have worked on international problems for a number of years they have come to know personally many governmental officials and members of the UN Secretariat. They can bring important concerns of the churches to the attention of these officers and, in fact, their counsel is frequently sought.

Lobbies are maintained in magnificent quarters near UN headquarters in New York. All the clerics who want to dress in striped pants and beribboned waistcoats and tell the international bureaucrats how to run their business can do so. They are continually finding reasons for trips around the world at church expense to help Vietnam conclude an armistice, to solve labour disputes at Geneva, to settle racial tensions in South Africa, to promote UNESCO projects in Timbuktu, and what not. The Council undoubtedly has proper uses in the international political melange — but the way it is being run today brings discredit upon World Christendom.

The Communist "party line" is frequently advanced by Council pronouncements and actions. As a part of its "coexistence" policy the Council has endorsed the admittance of Red China to the United Nations. Council members have been urged to help "create conditions" which would permit the 650,000,000 citizens of "the People's China" to have a voice in world affairs.

There is probably no more diabolic example of communist totalitarian evil than Mao Tse-tung's domain. Its communes have broken up family life and imposed a system of state slavery. Honor, honesty and human dignity have been destroyed. Christian missionaries have been tortured and slaughtered. Churches that will not accept government control and teach a communistic gospel have been closed since 1950. Mao has threatened the whole world with destruction if it falls to accept the communist way of life.

Yet the WCC counsels not only admittance to the UN but recognition by all governments and the establishment of diplomatic relations. It seems to be entirely unmindful that every such concession immediately benefits the power growth of world communism and weakens the world-wide influence of Christianity.

So far has the Council gone in its soft policy on communism that it advocates the communist doctrine of "peaceful coexistence." It is ironical that this slogan, originated by Josef Stalin himself, should be solemnly proposed in a body of Christians as the basis of relations with Russia, China and their satellite powers. Every state which has accepted the principle has been swallowed up by the Red community of nations. Most vigorous proponents of the idea are pacifists who believe that the only alternative is a war which might destroy civilization. Middle-of-the-road advocates feel that all-out opposition to communism would be too negative — "we should be for something, not *against*." Reds are 100 per cent for the policy.

Coexistence means economic, political and ideological conflict until such time as the enemies of communism have been reduced to a condition which will make the inevitable war a certain victory for the Reds. The Communist

International is now ready to move into every
new open area, prepared to demonstrate the
superiority of the communist social and governmental order, ideology and morality. Communist promotion of "coexistence" is in itself
intensified warfare. Agreement to it is surrender to the activities of trained political agitators, terrorists, local Communist party organizations and Communist front groups.

It remained for the 1961 New Delhi (India) Assembly of the World Council to finally cement
its cordial relations with Red communism. Here
the Russian Orthodox Church was received as a
full-fledged member along with several other
churches from Iron Curtain lands. The Russian
church is Communist-controlled and is a major
part of the world communist conspiracy.

When the Reds first came to power in Russia,
the Eastern Orthodox Church resisted communism. Its Patriarch Tikhon was murdered by
the Reds because of his loyalty to the Christian
faith. Today the Orthodox in Russia is a "kept"
church. Patriarch Alexi, elevated in 1945, received his office with the approval of the Soviet
state. Georgi G. Karpov, chairman of the Council
of Affairs of the Orthodox Church, is a major
general of the secret police. Metropolitan Nikodim is Karpov's agent charged with carrying out
the will of the state.

When invitations were originally sent out to all
churches inviting them to come to Amsterdam in
1948 for the organization of the World Council,
Dr. W. A. Visser t'Hooft, the general secretary,
and other prominent leaders, did everything they
could to get the Russian Church to enter the
ecumenical fold. It is interesting to note that its
Red leaders declined on the grounds that "the
practical aim of the Ecumenical Movement today

is . . . to turn aside from its seeking of the Kingdom of God and enter a political arena which is
foreign to its purpose". They said the Council
was an "effort by means of social and political
activity to create an Ecumenical Church as an
international influence" which they could not
endorse. In other words, they then saw the Council as a rival and a threat to the communist
conspiracy.

Subsequently, Dr. Eugene Carson Blake* and
nine American church leaders softened up the
Moscow Patriarchate by a visit to Russia in
1956. The declaration of the Evanston Assembly
(1958) on world peace and disarmament made a
considerable appeal to the Red delegates present
and is believed to have been the opening wedge
that led to a change of attitude toward the Council.
The same year at Utrecht, exchanges of visits
and information between the WCC and Russian
Church unofficial representatives was agreed
upon. In 1959 an international delegation of WCC
staff members, led by Dr. Visser t'Hooft, went to
the Soviet Union for a serious conference with
Patriarch Alexi, Metropolitan Nikodim and other
high officers of the Church. They returned much
encouraged. Russian Orthodox representatives
thereafter appeared in meetings of the Faith and
Order Commission, the executive committee of
the Commission of the Churches on International
Affairs, and the WCC Central Committee. His
Holiness the Patriarch of Moscow sent a cordial
greeting to the meeting of the Committee at Saint
Andrews, Scotland (1960), and was officially represented by two observers, Professor Vitaly
Borovoy and Mr. Victor Alexeey. Then there
were visits to World Headquarters at Geneva
where operations of the Council were minutely
studied and evaluated. No such thorough inves-

tigation had ever been made in all the history of
the Council. The Russian Church and the Soviet
government now knew more about WCC operations than most of its members. The Reds were
evidently not only satisfied but enthusiastic about
the possibilities of membership for the Russian
Church because they appeared at Buck Hill Falls,
Pennsylvania, in April, 1961, to make official
application in the name of the Holy Synod. Of
course, New Delhi approved amid great rejoicing.

With the entry of the Russian Church (50 million members), the Bulgarian Church (6 million
members), the Rumanian Church (13 million
members), and the Polish Church (400 thousand
members), the Eastern Orthodox constituency in
the Council was boosted to nearly 100 million.
The Eastern Orthodox churches with 17 members on the Central Committee now constitute the
largest confessional segment in the Committee,
which is the authoritative policy-determining,
program-making, and action-directing body of
the organization. Coupled with other Catholic-
type churches (such as the Anglican, Old Catholic, Coptic, Mar-Thoma, and the newly formed
nationalistic ecumenical churches such as the
Church of South India), this means that the Council has definitely broken away from its original
Protestant anchorage and its Western heritage to
swing increasingly farther and farther toward
the Catholic orbit.

Coincidental with the reception of the Russian
Orthodox Church, the Council in effect welcomed
Red communism into its fellowship. Naive Council leaders insist that there was nothing political
about the event. They rejoice in what they call
the achievement of a united Christian witness
unhampered by East-West political and ideological cleavages. They say that the cause of "peace

with justice and freedom" has been greatly advanced and that Christianity will be vastly
strengthened in Iron Curtain lands. With the
Muscovites given representation at New Delhi
on sections, study groups, and committees, they
kept the Council from making any derogatory
statements about communism and influenced the
decision to ask recognition of Red China by the
United Nations. Dr. O. Frederick Nolde of the
CCIA welcomed representatives of the Red
churches to his commission and felt that it
could now move with greater speed toward
"breaking the rigidity of United States policy
on people-to-people relations" which member
churches of the WCC hold and advocate about the
social order and national and international life.
With communist help Dr. Nolde anticipated radical changes which could soon bring meaningful
consensus. He expected and got strong support
from the Russians for his own views on disarmament, nuclear testing, a better deal for Red
China, and revolutionary changes in the social
order.

From Moscow has come the word that Metropolitan Nikodim is the man who will "call the
turns" for the Russians in the Council. What
Russia does will have a strong influence upon
its satellite churchmen in the Iron Curtain countries. Patriarch Alexi is only a figurehead. The
Red personnel on the commissions and committees are mere puppets. Nikodim has long
collaborated with Soviet authorities to keep the
Church under government control and a supple
instrument in its hands. He is the man who arranged for the absorption into the Church of
numerous MGB agents who later became bishops.
He supervised the brutal purging of non-
communist elements in the Church in Ukrania.

His official church publication has so vigorously propagandized against American and the West that at one time it was barred from the U. S. mails. Nikodim will make no move, and he will permit his underlings to make no move without the approval of high echelons of the Soviet government and the Communist Party. Only the naive can believe that no ulterior Soviet purpose is involved in permitting the Russian Church to join the World Council of Churches.

What is the meaning of this development to Protestantism and particularly to those American Protestant churches which are members of the World Council? No finer answer can be found than that made by Dr. Emil Brunner, one of the world's most noted theologians. Writing in the *Neue Zurcher Zeitung* of Zurich, Switzerland, he said recently, "So it has come about that there is a growing realignment with communism with constant stress and effort to learn to understand one another in a brotherly fashion. Recently this thought has been introduced through ecumenical channels into the churches of the United States ... This poison which paralyzes the will to resist, something the American people has been immune to up to now, is becoming virulent in America. Thus the Church without at all being communist, is unwittingly doing the work of communism. . . Because the people of the West still live in a world where thinking for oneself and expressing these thoughts are a matter of course, they are quite incapable of imagining a generation of humanity so completely inhuman. For this reason they still permit themselves to defame anti-communism as willful, inhuman, and unChristian, and even indulge the luxury of fighting anti-communism. It is indeed high time to awake from this madness and rise up so that we may protect

mankind, ourselves, our children, and our grandchildren from this ghastly end which will nullify
the fruits of all history of man. . . The extin-
guishing of the free spirit and the soul of man is
too high a price to pay for social and political
progress."

American Protestants numbering 30 million
have refused to associate themselves with the
World Council. They contend that (1) it rejects
an absolute minimum of Biblical doctrine as a
basis for true Christian fellowship, (2) it is
controlled by a liberal theological and sociological oligarchy, (3) it is beginning to function as a
"Super Church", threatening the freedom of Protestant churches, (4) it is destroying distinctly
evangelical Christian missions, (5) it is becoming more Catholic than Protestant, (6) it is encouraging leftist social revolution, meddling in
national and international politics thus imperil-
ling the status of the churches and the peace of
the world, and (7) it is blurring the obligation of
the Church Universal to maintain its apostolic-
ity in doctrine, ordinances, and life by its emphasis on Christian unity for unity's sake and the
building of One Church for One World.

Worldwide co-operative bodies, such as the
World Evangelical Fellowship (25 million members) and the International Council of Christian
Churches (5 million members) have been organized in recent years to serve conservative
Protestants outside the WCC and they are enjoying rapid growth.

The supreme tragedy of the World Council
situation is that it is promoting ignorance of the
content and message of the Holy Scriptures and
consequently their ethics. Without Scripture the
churches are being cast entirely upon the values
and goals of the contemporary world and being

brainwashed into believing that the world's hope lies in a secular Utopia. Politics has been substituted for the Gospel and the Zeitgeist for the Holy Spirit of God.

We have, for want of space, devoted this chapter mostly to Item 6. This then is the sad state of affairs resulting from the organization created largely through the efforts of the late Bishop Oxnam (see Chapter I). Whether this was his hope is not for us to say. Yet it cannot be surprising when one recognizes the wide variety of radical and Communist-front organizations to which he belonged, such as the People's Educational League; Internationale, extremely left-wing group led by Fannie Bixby Spencer; Federated Farm-Labor Party; National Council, Committee on Militarism in Education; Advisory Board, League for Organization of Progress; Fellowship of Reconciliation; American League Against War and Fascism; American Civil Liberties Union; National Council of American-Soviet Friendship; National Committee, Friends of Democracy; American Round Table on India, of which Louis Adamic, notorious radical was chairman.

Protestantism has and will continue to exist under various forms of social organization, but its true advocates strongly believe that the chief business of the Church is the preaching and teaching of the Biblical Gospel for the salvation of lost and sinful souls and for the moral and spiritual nurture of all followers of Christ. It is when the temporal welfare of human society becomes the major concern rather than the by-product of Christianity and when fateful compromises are made with godless ideologies that Protestantism must again become a protest. Many of us are convinced that the World Council of Churches now occupies dangerous ground through its pronouncements and actions in this area of its program and that it is no longer worthy of our support. A new era of evangelical Protestant action is imperative.

*Dr. Eugene Carson Blake, executive head of the United Presbyterian Church, U.S.A. was elected General Secretary (head) of the World Council of Churches on Feb. 11, 1965.

Rousas
John
Rushdoony

Chapter 10

HAS THE U.N.
REPLACED CHRIST
AS A WORLD RELIGION?

A Special Chapter for Clergymen

ROUSAS JOHN RUSHDOONY

Rousas John Rushdoony is the author of a number of books (*By What Standard?*, 1959, *Van Til* 1960, *Intellectual Schizophrenia* 1961, *The Messianic Character of American Education* 1963, *This Independent Republic* 1964, *Freud* 1965, *The Nature of the American System* 1965,) and pamphlets (*Translation and Subversion* 1964, *The Religion of Revolution* 1965, *The United Nations: A Religious Dream* 1965,) and a contributor to various journals and magazines.

Rushdoony is an ordained minister in the Orthodox Presbyterian Church and has held two pastorates as well as serving as a missionary among Chinese Americans, and Paiute and Shoshone Indians. He is an editor of the Philosphical and Historical Series, International Library of Philosophy and Theology. Rushdoony has served as an independent consultant to a foundation, been on the staff of a research institute, and has lectured extensively across the country. He is presently located in Woodland Hills, California, and devotes his full time to research, writing, and lecturing.

Rushdoony was born in New York City, April 25, 1916, but, except for several years in Detroit, Michigan, has resided mainly in California, and as a missionary to the Indians, in Nevada. He is a graduate of the University of California, B.S. and M.A., and of the Pacific School of Religion, B.D.

Philosophically, Rushdoony is a member of the school of throught known as presuppositionalism, whose major figure in the United States is Dr. Cornelius Van Til. Rushdoony's first two books deal specifically with Van Til's philosophy, and he is currently working on an extensive study, from this perspective, of a major problem of philosophical history.

The Messianic Character of American Education is an extensive analysis of the philosophies of education in the United States from Horace Mann to the present, the most thorough study of the subject yet made. *Intellectual Schizophrenia* also deals with educational philosophies. *This Independent Republic* and *The Nature of the AmericanSystem* are studies in American political philosophies and history.

In this chapter, Has the U. N. replaced Christ as a World Religion? Rushdoony has shown how the "gospel" of the churches came to be the U.N. rather than Jesus Christ, so that it became a religious imperative to work for the creation and support of the U.N.

HAS THE U.N. REPLACED CHRIST
AS A WORLD RELIGION?

A Special Chapter for Clergymen

by Rousas John Rushdoony

According to a noted historian,

> The nineteenth century has been given various names by historians, most often perhaps "the century of nationalism". One could just as well call it the century of internationalism, for the latter movement actually came into being in that century and had a very deep effect on its history.[1]

The term "the century of internationalism" is a good one for the nineteenth century, although Koht's reasons are the wrong ones. Koht was correct in tracing the roots of twentieth century internationalism to the major thinkers and leaders of the nineteenth century, but that century was an era of genuine internationalism for other reasons. True internationalism rests, not on ideas of world unity through world-wide political coercion, but on a free order wherein men, ideas, and goods can move freely across borders in terms of the liberty of all. Because the nineteenth century was more or less firmly committed to a hard money policy, to gold and silver, an internationalism of trade and travel prevailed. Transportation facilities were steadily extended throughout Europe, the Americas, Africa, and Asia, and trade penetrated the far corners of the world. Traders might have strongly nationalistic and racial ideas, but free trade and hard money were color blind and knew no frontiers. Men and goods travelled freely across

boundaries to a degree unknown to the mid-
twentieth century, and ideas followed them everywhere. The nineteenth century was also the great
era of missionary expansion by evangelical
Christianity, an internationalistic faith holding to
the salvation of all manners, classes, and colors
of men in the true church of Jesus Christ, and
congregations prayed for the conversion of the
heathen and received with joy the missionary
reports of the regeneration of previously depraved savages and idolators. One of the most
popular songs of the century, and the most
popular of all internationalistic songs, surpass-
ing perhaps even the Internationale in its history
and influence, was Reginald Heber's (1783-1826)
great missionary hymn:

> From Greeland's icy mountains,
>   From India's coral strand,
> Where Afric's sunny fountains
>   Roll down their golden sand,
> From many an ancient river,
>   From many a palmy plain,
> They call us to deliver
>   Their land from error's chain.
>
> Can we, whose souls are lighted
>   With wisdom from on high,
> Can we to men benighted
>   The lamp of life deny?
> Salvation! O salvation!
>   The joyful sound proclaim,
> Till each remotest nation
>   Has learnt Messiah's Name.
>
> Waft, waft, ye winds, His story,
>   And you, ye waters, roll,
> Till, like a sea of glory,
>   It spreads from pole to pole;
> Till o'er our ransomed nature
>   The Lamb for sinners slain,
> Redeemer, King, Creator,
>   In bliss returns to reign.

Millions knew these words by heart, sang them

weekly in Sunday School or church as a missionary offering was received, and thousands upon thousands went out as missionaries in a day
when being a missionary spelled sacrifice, hard-
ship, sickness and death, because they were
moved by a Christian internationalism, by a
desire to bring the unregenerate into salvation
and into Christian civilization. Schools and hos-
pitals were established by the missionaries, and
outstanding converts were sent to the homeland
to be trained in theology and in terms of Christian civilization in order to reproduce it in
Africa, Asia, and the Pacific islands.

This was internationalism, and this powerful
movement, combined with political and economic
liberty, made the nineteenth the century of internationalism. Men looked beyond their own frontiers, were moved by a sense of Christian responsibility for the eternal and material welfare
of others, and a genuine internationalism flourished. This internationalism did not dream of an
organic union of nations and a political order:
it did visualize a Christian world and free political orders and world-wide free economics.

Meanwhile, however, other forces were working for precisely this organic internationalism
and world state. From the French Revolution on,
international socialism, and later Marxist and
non-Marxist socialism, began to work for a
world of unity in terms of statist equality, usually an equality gained by the extermination of all
classes save one, the intellectually defined
"workers" class. This internationalism has no
sense of "brotherhood" beyond its ideologically
defined boundaries: it hates with passion all who
are outside the socialist camp, and it often hates
and kills its own socialist brethren. In terms of
this new "internationalism", the borders began

to close tightly, and the old free world began to resolve itself into a series of prison camps called socialist and welfare states.

Socialist internationalism became "scientific" because of Charles Darwin, whose theory of evolution gave Marxism the basis it needed. According to orthodox Christianity, God is the Creator and man the creature. In terms of evolution, man has evolved, has made himself blindly through struggle and natural selection. Scientific, socialist man can now remake and develop himself as never before. The clay has become the potter. Man can make of man the new god of being, the plastic and fully potential Adam of the socialist paradise. Socialism and science combined, not to subjugate nature primarily but to subjugate and to remake man after their ideal image. This dream, the humanist dream, deliberately seeks to replace the old Christian doctrines of salvation and internationalism with a man-centered dream. As a lecturer at the New School for Social Research stated it,

> The new order would be an order that, for the first time since the Holy Roman Empire, would comprehend the entire world and bring it into a state of peace and vital equilibrium. For the first time, it would again be an order that has the welfare of man for its all-important focus. In the Holy Roman Empire, this welfare was salvation, a purely spiritual welfare that rested in the hereafter, in the grace of God; soul and body were far apart, precisely as far as heaven and earth. The Kingdom of God and its ideal order floated high above man, and below, in the earthly realm of the emperor, that secular dynamism was in the making, which later rent the world in the struggle for power of dynasties, nations and economies and led it from crisis to crisis. Since that time man has come of age. He has cast off the authority of the church, and his coming of age is an irrevocable fact, no matter how immature he may be for the task of directing himself. The directive no longer comes only from above, it comes from below, not only from a Creator, but from a creation, from conditions that man has produced, without

knowing it or wishing it, in his mad chase for earthly goods. But men disregard the commands of their creation just as they disregarded the commandments of their Creator. In today's technological situation is hidden the same human significance that was revealed by the Word of God, only that today, the idea is no longer separate from matter. It is deeply and secretly incorporated in matter and so, for the first time, it may have the prospect of materializing. Pure ideas tend to become doctrines rather than reality. Nor will the new order be created by the pure idea, it will be tortured out of men through cruel and bitter necessity — how bitter, coming generations alone may know.[2]

In the Christian perspective, the government is upon God's shoulders; He creates, predestines, and governs, and the world is under God's providence. In the humanistic perspective, the government is upon man's shoulders; man makes himself, predestines his own being, controls and governs the world as total planner, and the world is placed under man's providence.

Humanism has been defined by A. J. Bahm in D. D. Runes' *Dictionary of Philosophy* as "Any view in which interest in human welfare is central." While more specific definitions exist, this is the general meaning of the term. Human welfare is central and most important in every kind of humanism and takes precedence over the laws of God and of man. The consistent humanist cannot give anything priority over human welfare, because nothing is more important for him than man. Moreover, consistent humanism defines human welfare without any reference to and standard outside of man's reasoning or desiring.

In the United States, this man-centered emphasis found first and decisive expression in the Unitarian and Universalist movements and rapidly infected all churches with this dedicated humanism. The Abolitionist movement was a product of this humanism, or the religion of humanity, and it demanded the Civil War as the first stage in world revolution. The Rev. Mondure Daniel Conway (1832-1907) termed the Civil War "a rebellion vs. a revolution" and "a war for humanity", for "the Republic of man".[3] Rev. Octavius Brooks Frothingham (1822-1895) stated what the Civil War as revolution meant to him and his fellow humanists: "the reconstruction of a new order, on the basis of freedom for mankind, was the first installment of the Messianic Kingdom."[4] At the beginning of the twentieth century, another humanist emphasized the same point:

America did not spend a million lives of men for the sake of transferring the sovereignty of state from Richmond to Washington. The Civil War was the revolt of the people against the priests of politics; it defied the constitution and flouted every rite of legalism to free slaves. The Civil War was a revolution.[5]

The Rev. Charles Ferguson (b. 1863) received high praise for *The Religion of Democracy* from the Rev. Charles H. Parkhurst, the Rev. T. T. Munger, the Rev. Philip Moxom, the Rev. George Hodge, dean of the Episcopal Theological School, Cambridge, Massachusetts, and from Edwin Markham, Julian Hawthorne, and Ella Wheeler Wilcox, among other. The Arena reviewer, calling it an "inspiring book, dominated by a broad and deeply religious spirt," added that "I have seldom read a work that so bristles with virile thought."[6] Charles Ferguson was for a time rector of St. James' Church, Syracuse, New York. He was also a member of the New York bar, and for some years an editorial writer for the Hearst newspapers.[7] In the year prior to World War I, Ferguson "was employed by the United States government to find how 'big business' stood to the state in the principal European countries" and carried credentials from the president.[8] *The Religion of Democracy* sold widely and was favorably received, with little awareness of its radically subversive nature. Its humanism and internationalism were accepted as "idealism" and as the logical development and evolution of Christianity and all noble purposes in humanity. The Rev. Charles Ferguson lashed out at the Christian and American past, and at God-centered religion. "The America of the paper constitution" had to go; his faith, "big with revolution", was in a man-centered universe, in which "The soul is the concrete absolute."[9] Man is "of the same stuff as God",[10] and "there is only one sovereignty, and its extraterritoriality is, for this day, in your own body".[11] Since man is the absolute, man is the judge rather than the judged. "The propositions of the spirit are not on trial, but the world is on trial."[12] Is the world fit and ready to be a habitation for sovereign and absolute man? For Ferguson, "The new century opens with great expectancy. The future is full of charm."[13] The dead past would soon be discarded:

A few more battles fought from habit and momentum, and European armies that confront each other with so grim and threatening an aspect will laugh out loud at the credulity of their masters, and fling themselves into each other's arms.[14]

Liberty, fraternity, and equality shall prevail.[15] Democracy will command the future as "The Revolution Absolute", and evolution will culminate in revolution: "The object becomes subject, the thing made becomes maker; the clay becomes potter."[16] This is the essence of it, *the clay becomes potter*, man remakes himself and his world. Man, in "the new order", identifies himself with God, "and his freedom is, like God's, to get into the creation." [17] Political democracy is a failure. "Democracy. . . as a balloting contrivance" is not true democracy but "an ingenious futility." [18] The new order will begin in America, "the land of the incarnation" of flux:

This shall be the land of change, flux, progress; everything must flow. We will have nothing fixed and settled — not the ribs of the earth nor the anatomy of a man. [19]

A few things were, however, fixed for Ferguson: the sovereignty of man, and the oneness of humanity. [20] Man would be one, moreover, in a "Democratic Catholic Church" as a branch of the State, the "disciplinary arm of the Church", which Church being "the people organized in liberty". [21] Three things shall characterize this world church and order. *First,* "The Church shall discover the eternal in the flesh," that is, in a material order:

It shall be disclosed that God has so framed this tangible world that it will respond only to the communion and unanimity of men . . . The building of the world-city will be seen to be the goal of history . . . The earth has possessed the people, and history has been mainly a gloss upon economics. The program of the new era is to put the people in possession of the earth — to put the whole people in possession of the whole earth. [22]

This is the true Church's program of "sacred and eternal secularity". *Second,* the Church will be universalist; all men as men, whether good or bad, will be members, for

the Church will utterly shatter the caste of goodness and definitely abandon the attempt to mark a distinction between good persons and the bad . . . The Church will refuse to exercise what is called spiritual discipline, and it will jealously guard its officers from the imputation of being particularly pious . . .

The Church will regard itself as constitutionally coterminous with secular society . . . [23]

Thus the Church and humanity will be identical

facts and concepts. *Third,* "the Church will abandon the attempt to truss up and underpin the
Truth"; rather, pragmatic developments will reveal truths, for "the Truth is not a sacred de-
posit to be kept in a box under guard of priestly
seneschals, but a living, tremendous Thing —
able to take care of Itself as well as of all who
will trust it".[24]

This is Ferguson's goal for man. For him
"original sin" is "the rejection of the human
ideal and the going in search of a non-human
law of good and evil."[25] Ferguson attacked "The
Superstition of Arbitrary Law"; his hope was in
man's law: "The soul sets out to impose itself
upon the universe with confidence that, in spite
of appearances, it is possible to do so; that the
constitution of the universe is not alien to the
soul".[26] Ferguson denied the validity of ballot-
box democracy. His democracy meant getting
"men to want congruous things, . . . a concurrence of desire".[27] "The perfect triumph of
democracy is to get the knaves to consent to the
jail and rejoice in it".[28] In modern terms, this
requires brainwashing; for Ferguson it was the
new order, attained, in his idealistic language,
by integration. "The integration of universal
society follows upon the integration of the individual soul."[29] This means destroying the old
solidarities of clans and races. "The old solidarity must be dissolved in order that the opposite principle, the principle of unanimity, may
be established. Democracy stakes everything on
the individual, because the individual is the
universal."[30] Since some men had to guide this
re-making of man, it would appear that for
Ferguson some men are more "universal" than
others!

For Ferguson, the university, to be truly a

university, had to dedicate itself to this humanistic ideal, not to an aristocratic culture. "As
the truth comes more and more to be thought
of as the sum of those urgent realities with which
we must wrestle in making ourselves a place in
the universe, the transcendentalism of learning
gives place to a frank pragmatism."[31] In terms
of this new faith, "The university must become a
militant order, a self-conscious and self-con-
fident army," whose purpose it is to "sweep out
of men's minds the superstitions of arbitrary
and conventional law."[32] The goal is a truly human and humanistic order. *"The Artistic-
Scientific Republic is the true Church."*[33] Moreover, *"The advance to a material civilization,
more refined, more various and more free, requires that the church, the university, and the
political primary shall be telescoped into a single
institution."*[34]

Ferguson believed in a government of men in
terms of humanism, not a government of laws:

Let it be repeated and insisted upon that it is scholastic
platonism to declare that we are bound to have a government, "not of men, but of laws", and thereupon to set to
work with all diligence to clear the unsophisticated human-
ness out of everybody who has to do with the administration
of the legal system.[35]

Adam fell because "He insisted upon having a
Constitution, before going to work. His Business
was to be subjected to a transcendental
Politics."[36] Man must become his own god and
world-maker. "It is in the power of the Man to
pass out of the realm of creaturehood and into
the realm of creatorship. He can cease to be
merely the Finest Thing Made, and can become
the Maker of Things."[37]

Ferguson was not alone in such thinking. Thousands of books from the Civil War era through

World War I reflected this same humanism in varying degrees. Not only the spokesmen of religious liberalism but those of evangelical Christianity revealed their humanism to a startling degree. The primary task of Christianity, for the evangelicals, ceased to be obedience to and the enjoyment of God but rather the "saving of souls". Revivalism decried doctrinal differences and clear statements in theology; these God-centered concerns were deemed irrelevant in comparison to the all-important and man-centered task of "soul-saving". Ferguson had reasoned some of the implications of his position more than others, but his premises were common to his day, and they gained easy and ready approval.

Because the intellectual climate of the day was so congenial to this religious humanism, the Federal Council of the Churches of Christ in America, in its inception in 1908, was not viewed as a radical step, as later conservatism was to see it, but as a cautious but necessary step for the churches. It had been preceded, in its function, by various organizations, such as the Open and Institutional Church League, and the National Federation of Churches and Christian Workers. The Federal Council had its origin in the social gospel: the dream of "federal unity" for the churches "came from men who were wrestling with the practical tasks of the churches in what was becoming a hostile or increasingly unaccommodating social order."[38] The Federal Council, in its Plan of Federation, excluded from its jurisdiction "authority over the constituent bodies adhering to it" as part of its strictly federal nature, and, theologically, avoided and denied its authority "to draw up a common creed or form of government or of worship". Its central and most specific functions were *ecumenicity* and the *social gospel*:

To express the fellowship and catholic unity of the Christian Church. . . To secure a larger combined influence for the churches of Christ in all matters affecting the moral and social condition of the people, so as to promote the application of the law of Christ in every relation of human life.[39]

Two things were clearly apparent in this and subsequent Federal Council, and, later, National Council, statements. *First,* the unity of the churches is seen in terms of humanism rather than theological primacy; it is man-centered rather than God-centered. Its concern is with social order, not theological order, and its projected social order is humanistic, not theocentric. It may speak of building the Kingdom of God, but it clearly means the Kingdom of Man and the unity of man. *Second,* the Reformation principle has been abandoned. The Reformers longed for and cherished unity, but, in the final analysis, they insisted on truth above unity rather than a compromise of truth. The churches of twentieth century America, deeply infected by pragmatism, steadily down-graded truth in the name of unity, so that unity came to be not only higher than truth but a kind of substitute god. By 1962, Justice Douglas could write, with only minor disenting voices, of America's goal, that "Truth is not the goal, for in most areas no one knows what truth is."[40]

Meanwhile, theological developments had further emphasized the development of humanism within the churches. Barthianism, ostensibly a reaction against humanism, was actually a development of it. By driving a deep wedge between the Christ of faith and the Jesus of history, neo-orthodoxy further surrendered the church to the affairs of time if it was to be at all relevant to this world. God is made "totally other" and is read out of this world, if not out of existence, so that man is left free to dominate history in terms of his own will. The close affinity of neo-orthodoxy to socialism is no accident: it is a product of the substitution of the predestination by man the planner for predestination by God. For a neo-orthodoxy theologian to be other than a Socialist is an act of inconsistency. Cornelius Van Til has identified the radical humanism of Barth and Brunner:

Both have been particularly insistent that God meets man and man meets God only in Christ, and that Christ stands for the Individual in whom all distinctions are correlative to one another. As the chief interpretative category of dialecticism, the Individual takes the place of the ontological trinity in orthodox theology; in it being is exhausted in relation and relation is exclusively internal.[41]

In such theologies, as well as those of Tillich, Reinhold Niebuhr, and others, God was essentially no more than a limiting concept. In Tillich's disciple, John A. T. Robinson, Bishop of Woolwich, and author of *Honest to God* and *The New Reformation?*, even the formality of God began to disappear.

In the "Death of God" school of theology, the formality of God was entirely dropped for a forthright and total humanism. The starting point of this school is that *God is dead,* for the time "has arrived to engage in a radical quest for a new mode of religious understanding. The first requirement of such a quest is the forthright confession of the death of the God of Christendom."[42]

This "post-Christian" perspective is far more pervasive than the formal "Death of God" school of theology. Its premises are native to the current theological scene. Thus, Dr. Gerald Jud, chief of evangelism for the United Church of Christ, has stated, "The world has changed, but the church hasn't. We must rebuild ourselves around man's problems. This Reformation is more far-reaching than the first one." One pastor in San Francisco has echoed Ferguson's concept of the church:

The church once said, "Here we are — anytime you conform to our standards, we will let you join us." But people who are frightened or alone aren't ready for theology or rules. The church, at its best, reaches out to everybody and represents, regardless of race or creed, youth or age, the fellowship that is the gift of God.[43]

But a fellowship without creed is fellowship in terms of man, a humanistic fellowship, and humanistic fellowship is the new religion of the churches. "Said a proper Philadelphia lady, 'I was born again in Selma.' "[44] The religion she was "born again" into was humanism. The line of separation between the church and the world was steadily being destroyed. The church joined the world on the picket lines of "human rights". With a determined humanism, the church began to make terms with homosexuals, adulterers, law-breakers, and all others save orthodox Christians and conservatives. Like other crusading humanists, they saw themselves "as a kind of super-government without portfolio, and everybody else is expected to yield to them and get out of their way". In an April 19, 1965, *Chicago Tribune* editorial, it was noted that, "Of 441 persons arrested in recent street disturbances here, 61 of the adult males — 26 per cent — were clergymen."[45]

The reason was an obvious one: *the cause is man, the creed is man, and the gospel is the oneness of man.* Dr. Edmund P. Clowney of Westminster Seminary, in commenting on the

United Presbyterian Church's "Confession of 1967", stated,

The urgency of the church's mission according to the new confession is therefore not to plead with lost sinners, 'Be ye reconciled to God', but to promote the reconciliation of estranged races and nations.[46]

This, then, is the new gospel, the reconciliation of man to man, of race to race, and of creed to creed, the oneness of man and the unity of man apart from any rule of truth. This has been the gospel of most churches for almost a century, and their theologies have required the creation of an institution such as the United Nations Organization. The institutional relationship of the churches to the U.N. is a very real one, but, more than the institutional tie-in, the doctrinal tie-in is the closest and the most decisive one. The United Nations is the messiah that modern theology and preaching has long been calling into existence. It is the new god and savior of men who have declared the God of Scripture to be dead. The U.N. is their new source of final law, world unity and planning, their universal shepherd and source of peace. The churches who made it now bow down in worship before it. More than any other single factor, the churches are responsible for the United Nations. It has been their teaching and preaching which made it a "natural" and easy step for mankind, a "logical evolution" in world political order.

The Roman Catholic Church was also a part of this same movement, and Pope John XXIII's *Pacem in Terris* brought into the open long powerful trends. Catholics began to complain that the western world had become "more catholic" than the Church, and the church must seek this new catholicity.[47] One leader stated, "The problems of today are such that they can only be adequately settled by an international community of nations."[48] One Jesuit scholar opposed segregation on the grounds of "man's intrinsic worth" and stated "that a man has a right to honor simply on the grounds of his humanity",[49] grounds more suggestive of Kant and Ritschl than of orthodox Christianity. Another Jesuit, writing on ecumenism, substituted that word for Paul's *agape* (love, or charity), to declare:

Ecumenism is patient, is kind; ecumenism does not envy, is not pretentious, is not puffed up; is not ambitious, is not self-seeking, is not provoked; thinks no evil, does not rejoice over wickedness; but rejoices with the truth; bears with all things, believes all things, hopes all things, endures all things.[50]

One might add that ecumenism believes and endures all things save the gospel.

In Vatican Council II, the boundaries of unity were pressed very far in some speeches. Thus, Sergio Mendez Arceo, Bishop of Cuernavaca, Mexico, asked the Church to be "an Open Community": "The Church should be clearly presented as the sacrament of unity in the world as the Eucharist is the sacrament of unity in the Church". The Church must bring unity to the world.

And do not say that this is no longer Christian ecumenism. The goal of ecumenism is, by the witness of our own faith, to seek unity with those who give us a witness to their own religion. It is a unity of hearts which is to lead to a unity of minds in the whole earth.[51]

Among those to be included in the new ecumenism are the Jews, and the Freemasons, and penalities against Freemasons should be reappraised as "contrary to the Lord's teaching that the weeds should be left so as not to root up the wheat at the same time".[52] According to Cardinal Bea, the unity of the Church and the unity of mankind are related concepts.

Nevertheless, a basic question still remains: are there two unities to be regarded as permanently different and divided, admitting and encouraging mutual collaboration, but still remaining separate, or are they to be considered as converging lines, having a dynamic tendency to meet together? This is to ask whether the natural principles and forces which unite men in a common nature stand, as many think, independent of the religious problem. It is to ask whether the great world religions — Animism, Confucianism, Hinduism, Buddhism, Judaism, Christianity, Mohammedanism — are to continue until the end of time, having at the most tolerance toward each other; or whether there is, by God's planning and mysterious designs, a dynamic of history which tends towards an ultimate merging between the natural and the religious unity of the human family?[53]

Cardinal Bea seems to favor this grand merging and unity, but, because this is heretical ground in part, he treads carefully. The Christian unity differs for Bea because it rests on a form of deification, "a new communication of God's very being to men"; the Christian becomes " 'deified' by baptism" while still remaining man. On the other hand, non-Christians too have a baptism. Besides baptism of water there is what is called 'baptism of desire', consisting in a willingness to do what God wants . . . Pope Alexander VIII in 1690 condemned the assertion that 'pagans, Jews, heretics and suchlike people have not sufficient grace.' "[54] Bea thus opened the door to universalism and to unity as the supreme goal for mankind. Not surprisingly, the first appendix to his book is the text of the U.N. Universal Declaration of Human Rights.

The vision then is of world unity and of world peace. It is a vision of world peace also, we are told, but "It is well to remember that it is not the world, itself, which is to be disarmed and strictly controlled — but people who live in it."[55]

The Federal Council of Churches greeted the birth of the U.N. with joy, and the U.N. Charter was approved "within 24 hours after the close of the United Nations Conference on International Organization at San Francisco" in 1945. Approving of the "humanitarian aims set forth in the preamble," it declared that "The will to cooperate requires as a foundation, a new international morality."[56]

The new and saving order had arrived, and "a new international morality," based on the premise of the oneness and sovereignty of man, was the gospel of the day. The social gospel had done its work; it was now time for social action: The world must be disarmed, and the United Nations made the world government. Nationalism and national independence must be destroyed. A world law and a world court must have prior jurisdiction. All barriers of nation and immigration must be steadily smashed in the name of the new morality. Racial integration must be furthered because the unity and amalgamation of races is supremely good. Local civil governments and the strength of local roots must give way to "greater loyalties". All men as men have equal right apart from their character, condition, education, or any other factor, and any form of differentiation or discrimination is evil. This and much more, including a new sexual morality, is the new international morality of social action. Man is made sovereign, and no moral law is recognized which stands in judgment over men and discriminates between them. In the words of the Rev. Charles Ferguson, "the clay becomes potter", man now becomes his own god and maker. Man becomes his own savior and effects "Reconciliation through self-offering."[57]

The churches have indoctrinated their mem-

bers into this faith, and they have been extensively supported by their membership. Much is made
of the unrest in the churches by some reporters,
but the unrest is mainly a minor one, a rebellion
at particular points where someone's private
ox is gored. In the main, most church members
are content to remain in their clearly humanistic churches with only minor protests. Sep-
arating churches have had only limited successes, usually limited to strong personalities
who command a following. A general stand in
terms of principles is lacking. Most church
members differ from their clergy only in degree,
not in kind: their faith is equally humanistic but
not as militantly consistent as the faith of the
clergy. Church members hold to a humanism of
ease, to a man-centered faith in which God's
chief end is man's happiness and material welfare. Their conception of God is of a cosmic
Santa Claus. The clergy hold to a crusading and
consistent humanism. But the logic of both positions calls for a one-world order. The most surprising thing about the United Nations is that it
did not come sooner. The coming of the United
Nations was not a trick of politicians but a religious necessity, called into being by the religious humanism of the Western world. The work
of Alger Hiss in the formation of the U.N., and
of subversives within the churches, would have
been futile if the theological climate had not
favored them. The roots of the United Nations are
in religious humanism, and the U.N. will flourish
in spite of all its abject failures as long as these
roots remain strong. Only a return to orthodox
Christianity can shatter the messianic humanism
of the United Nations.

Meanwhile, true internationalism is perishing.
The internationalism of trade and money is wan-

ing, and the Christian missionary movement is being replaced by church-trained social workers, U.N. agencies, and U.S. Peace Corpsmen. Moreover, as national currencies grow weaker, and inflation and socialism increase, the rise of foreign exchange controls is everywhere in evidence. The outflow of capital, investments, loans, and the use of gold and silver is controlled. Tourists are limited in the amount of imports they can carry home without tax. Foreign trade, eagerly desired by all nations, decreases as socialism controls foreign trade and transactions. As a result, the twentieth century, dedicated to political and economic internationalism by treaties and market agreements, is becoming the century of economic nationalism. Moreover, the more the controls increase on the national and international level, the more the local units will contract in order to preserve themselves, for enforced internationalism robs a locality in the name of humanity and drives each area to protective isolationism. The steady deterioration of paper currencies again breaks down internationalism. Fiat money will not travel far, and the more a people are made dependent on it, the more rapidly will their isolation from the world be affected.

But, most of all, the humanism of the U.N. and of socialist internationalism means isolation from God and the certainty of His judgment. By creating in the U.N. a modern Tower of Babel, religious humanism has incured for itself the judgment of God, a scattering of man, and a new confusion of tongues and a confusion of faces. "Except the LORD build the house, they labour in vain that build it" (Psalm 127:1).

Charles S.
Poling

Chapter 11

What one Minister did
and a Challenge to all

CHOOSE YOU THIS DAY

CHARLES S. POLING

Dr. Charles S. Poling has come to be recognized as one of the leaders of that valiant company of Christian patriots who are carrying on an unremitting crusade against the socialistic, liberal invasion of the Christian church and our national government. His "Prepared Statement," blasting the National Council of Churches, delivered from the pulpit of the First Presbyterian Church of Phoenix, Arizona, February 12th, 1961 attracted world-wide attention and was the inspiration for the organization of the National Committee of Christian Laymen. Recently, on February 17th, 1964, Dr. Poling withdrew from membership in the United Presbyterian Church, U.S.A. He then helped establish a new church, The Church of all Christian Faiths, which is growing rapidly. The Poling family has played an active role in the religious life of America. Two of Dr. Poling's grandfathers were ministers. His father, Dr. Charles C. Poling was a minister and college president. His brother, Dr. Daniel A. Poling, is a minister and editor of *Christian Herald*. Dr. Charles Poling has been pastor of several of the larger churches of the Presbyterian denomination. He has preached in pulpits all over America as well as in Canada, Oxford and London, England. He is recognized as an authority on the American Constitution and has lectured on it in many cities of the United States. Dr. Poling served as Chaplain in both World War I and World War II. He has served as an active pastor for fifty years and is presently in great demand as preacher and lecturer in churches and colleges throughout the nation.

What one Minister did and a Challenge to all

CHOOSE YOU THIS DAY

by Charles S. Poling

On February 17, 1964, I withdrew from the United Presbyterian Church, U.S.A. I am no longer a member of that communion. Until these late years I walked straight and proud to be numbered among the ministers of this great church. I was proud of her history; proud of her uncompromising position in support of fundamental, Bible truth and doctrine; proud of her evangelistic fervor and her pulpit giants who commanded the respect of men and the favor of God. But Satan is cunning and subtle. While we basked in the glory that was our Presbyterian church, he fashioned a disguise, and lo, one day we awoke to find that we were occupied and taken over by his apostate, socialistic, political National Council of Churches.

The record of the NCC take-over of the United Presbyterian Church is the record of the NCC take-over of every member-church of the National Council. It is hard to believe that all this could take place without the consent, generally speaking, of the rank and file of our ministers and laymen. A few church leaders maneuvered a coup and the take-over was final and complete.

I admit that for a number of years I was deeply concerned because I recognized a definite drift toward liberalism. More recently I came alive to the fact that we had placed socialistic theological liberals at the head of our theological seminaries and these were sending forth a crop more atheistic than theistic.

As chairman of my Presbytery's Committee on Ministerial Relations, I received the applications of ministers who were seeking work within our Presbytery. I was concerned when I discovered so many newly ordained young men were stating that their chief interest was in the field of counseling — not preaching — young men with no ministerial experience and very little experience with life and its complexities presuming to counsel and advise people of maturity and experience. But I could not believe that the trend toward apostasy and socialism was as serious as it appeared. I reasoned that we were going through a phase in a changing world and would eventually find our way and return to proclaim His truth and witness to His Gospel.

But in place of growing better, things became worse. The enemy was more deeply entrenched than many of us had dreamed. Our executives, and all too many of our pastors, rose to take the bait of the so-called Social Gospel. The preaching of Christ and His cross began to fade from the pulpit scene. Many of us reasoned that by remaining with our church we could more effectively oppose the apostate forces than we could by withdrawing.

We engaged in an active campaign to alert our laymen to the mad scheme to destory our church per se and to have her absorbed in a massive One-World Protestant Church that, theologically, would be neither fish nor fowl, actually, no church at all.

I accused our liberals of transferring their

loyalty and devotion from God to the NCC. But the liquidation of the true and historic Presbyterian church has been in the making for more years than some of us care to admit. And what is true of the United Presbyterian Church is true of all churches presently members of the NCC. During recent years it seems that our church has grasped every opportunity to ally herself with the Godless forces of evil. She has ceased to behave and react as a Christian church when forced to take a position upon moral, social, and religious questions. All too often we find her uniting with Godless and violent forces, bringing shame and reproach upon the church of Jesus Christ.

Our 175th General Assembly in Des Moines, Iowa last May voted to express displeasure at prayers, religious observances, religious holidays, Christian scenes and Bible reading in the schools and on school property. This Assembly also disapproved tax exemption for churches — this has been Dr. Blake's baby. This Assembly also came out against Sunday closing laws. All of which means that we have a church crusading for a secular State, a State from which official recognition of God is removed. And let me remind you that this action was taken *before* the Supreme Court made its decision.

Through General Assembly's action, we joined hands and hearts with Mrs. Madalyn Murray of Baltimore, the atheist whose case against public school devotions was sustained by the Supreme Court. Do you think our action may have given aid and comfort to this character? What sort of a woman is Mrs. Murray that the highest court of America should surrender to her will while outraging the lofty ideals and historic traditions of the citizens of this great Republic? Hear this

gentle lady speak. I quote: "If I can't come
through this case the same offensive, unlovable,
bull-headed, defiant, aggressive slob that I was
when I started it, then I'll give up now. My
own identity is more important to me. They
can keep their g-d (she spelled it out) prayers
in the public schools, in public out-houses, in
public H-bomb shelters and in public # % *"
(Here she uses the most obscene name of a
public house.)

When we openly join forces with characters
such as this, can we — dare we — appeal to God
to strengthen and lead us? Our church leaders
use every known device to capture our laity for
the cause of socialistic theological liberalism.
Our church media — *Presbyterian Life, Monday
Morning,* and *Social Education and Action* —
dance merrily along assuming that all Presbyterians are liberals. These have become nothing
more than propaganda vehicles to further the
cause of socialism and apostasy. We find Dr.
Eugene Carson Blake, Clerk of our General
Assembly, leading so-called Freedom Marches
and playing patsy with one of the most notorious
pacifists and racial agitators in circulation today.
He shares the spotlight before the tomb of Lin-
coln with Bayard Rustin who has a record of 22
arrests and a conviction in 1953 on a morals
charge. (*Newsweek,* Sept. 2, 1963)

Many of our wisest and most earnest Christians are as eager as Dr. Blake to see all minority groups treated justly and given the same
freedoms and opportunities our own race enjoys.
However, they do not believe that the present
method of sit-downs and so-called Freedom
Marches accomplish the desired end.

Can the church command respect and loyalty
when her executives present a blasphemous mo-

tion picture as a part of the Protestant Center's World's Fair exhibit? The Committee responsible for the obscene exhibition is headed by a United Presbyterian executive, Dan Potter. In the film to be shown, Christ is depicted as a circus clown. Two prominent lay members of the committee resigned and on the eve of the opening of the Fair, president Robert Moses and his staff asked the Protestant Council to remove the film on the grounds of "grave misgivings" about "the propriety, good taste and validity of the film." But our modern Wise Men have an answer for simple lay folk. Churchman Dr. Potter told the Fair officials to stay out of the realm of religious film criticism. I repeat what I have often said: it's not the laymen that are rejecting the historic doctrines of our faith, not the layman that are leading us into the sin and darkness of apostasy, but the clergy.

And then parents began to come to me with obscene and sacreligious literature that their children and youth were being taught. "What shall we do now? Dr. Poling would you expose a small child of yours to this?" And I was forced to own that I would not. What kind of Christianity is this? How is it possible for us to get lost and worship the church and neglect our Christ? This happens and when it does happen we find it much easier to invite the unchurched to join our Church, than it is to invite them to surrender their lives to our Christ. Always and forever Christ must be preeminent and rule supreme in the Church. Loyalty to one's church is indeed a Christian grace but that loyalty must not degenerate into idolatry.

Multitudes have queried, "Dr. Poling, what can we do? We recognize the flagrant departure from orthodoxy by our pulpit; we are well aware that the apostate NCC has captured our churches and now presumes to speak for all Protestants of her member churches. We realize that our denominational leaders have surrendered functions and responsibilities to the NCC that no church should ever delegate or surrender. Tell us, just what can we do?"

Well, your prompt and positive action, as one Christian, may turn the tide of battle in Christ's favor. Eventually, there must be a general exodus whether you like that though or not. Until recently, I didn't like it and refused to entertain such an idea. I asked myself, "Suppose we put the NCC out of business tomorrow then just where do we stand?" The clergy that actually constitute the NCC are still in our pulpits preaching the same socialistic liberal doctrine. The seminaries that produce our new supply of ministers are still turning out young men who have been brainwashed and preach the liberal socialist line. Now where are we? Just where we have reposed in our stupor for so many unhappy years. Perhaps my recent experience will be of help to you.

I looked about and, with a shock, realized that as a member and minister of a church I knew to be apostate and, in too many instances, anti-Christ, I was standing among the enemies of my Lord. I saw myself as I have often looked at Peter, warming himself by the fire of the enemies of his Lord. I realized that I could not remain in His favor and enjoy His blessings if I continued to march with those who were opposing Him, questioning His birth, downgrading His Word, and collaborating with His enemies. My failure to actively oppose the evils I recognized made me a traitor to Him and His kingdom enterprise. I was sinning by my silence and haunted by the Scripture "He who knoweth to do right and doeth it not, to him it is sin."

It is not easy to break the ties of the years that have been the music and poetry of life to us and our children. But it is not easy to silently march with His foes and thus deny Him.

God is not dead, and neither is the power of His true church diminished. The church of Jesus Christ is immortal. It is a fellowship; it is an organism. It has a pulse, a heart, life. It has character and personality. You and I are the church in miniature. The forces of evil may destroy the visible church but the church of the living Christ is eternal and truly "will tower o'er the wrecks of time."

What can I do? Well, I cannot be the conscience of other men, but no matter what course others may decide to follow, I must do what His Spirit reveals to me to be right. For me to remain as His loyal disciple, for me to remain in His favor and know His fellowship, for me to walk in dignity and unashamed, there is but one course. As a Christian, I have no choice other than to separate myself from His foes and withdraw from a church that has been captured by liberal, socialistic leaders, a church that has transferred her devotion and loyalty from Christ to the apostate, anti-Christ, National Council of Churches.

But I cannot live as an island, I require the fellowship and encouragement of others. I cannot obey His command and fulfill my destiny by living a cloistered and selfish life. I must join His army and march with others of "like precious faith."

Thank God, there are still churches that have not "bowed the knee to Baal." There are churches not affiliated with the NCC. I am convinced that these have been raised up by our Lord "for such a time as this." Here are strong citadels of faith; here I will find a "city of refuge"; here, a fellowship where I can continue to bear my witness. These are days of decision for all Christians. We are forced to make the choice between Christ and a church that has been led into the ugly swamps of apostasy by her leaders. "No man can serve two masters," declared the Master of men. It is not possible for me to remain neutral. We cannot avoid getting involved. Whether we like it or not, we are involved and must make a choice. The choice? — Christ or the wicked forces of apostasy. If you be willing to serve the Lord, ". . . choose you this day whom ye will serve." (Joshua 24:15).

This is the action Dr. Poling has taken.

Below is the true and complete text of Dr. Poling's letter withdrawal from the United Presbyterian Church, U.S.A.:

February 17, 1964

The Rev. Claude L. Morton, Stated Clerk,
The Presbytery of Phoenix,
The United Presbyterian Church, U.S.A.

My dear Mr. Morton:

I am instructing you to erase my name from the roster of the ministers of the Presbytery of Phoenix, of the United Presbyterian Church, U.S.A.

I cannot longer give loyal support to a church that, through official action and pronouncements, unites with the forces of evil and goes on record as opposing the historic beliefs and doctrines that made us great and lent dignity and meaning to our preaching. I refer to the recent General Assembly's action relating to "public prayers, religious observances, religious holidays, Christian scenes, Bible reading in the schools and on school property; opposion to Sunday closing laws" and other deliverances one would expect atheistic groups to take but never such action from a church bearing the name and banner of our Lord and Saviour.

I cannot longer find fellowship in a church that blindly submits to the rule of Dr. Eugene Carson Blake who seems dominated by an omnipotent complex, associates with listed and known Communists, deliberately breaks the laws of a sovereign state, and leads marches that can only inspire hate and provoke violence. And I yield to no man in desire to see all minority groups enjoying the full and unrestricted blessings and opportunities my own race enjoys. When my church becomes the captive of the ultra liberal and apostate National Council of Churches, and the World Council and yields obedience to the socialistic, political heirarchy, my church can no longer claim my support and respect. I will not sin by remaining silent while my Presbytery considers becoming a member of the NAACP, a militant political organization. (See minutes of January meeting of Presbytery.)

Our denomination's news media — *Presbyterian Life, Social Education* and *Action,* and *Monday Morning* have been cap-

tured by the ultra Liberals and serve notice that there is
no place in the United Presbyterian Church, U.S.A., for
conservatives.

For nearly fifty years I have served my church and walked
proud and tall because I was counted worthy to be one of
her accredited ministers. There were "giants in the land"
in those days and they thundered God's truth as modern
Isaiahs. They "reasoned of righteousness, temperance, and
judgment to come." Today, when "the world at its worst
needs the church at its best," we get ourselves lost with the
lost. The great tragedy in ministerial circles today is that
the word "sin" is not held in repute, or even considered in
good taste. Now people make mistakes, have faults, fail to
achieve, suffer from complexes, are mentally ill. But sin?
No.

There is a crushing hand of shame upon me for my beloved
church, and a great sadness in my heart. I make my decision
after earnest prayer and the full concurrence of Mrs. Poling.
I shall continue my preaching into the future be that future
extended or brief, still preaching with pride and joy the Gospel proclaimed by our church Fathers throughout the years
of our glorious past.

                    Earnestly and sincerely,

                    CHARLES S. POLING

Howard E.
Kershner

Chapter 12

WHAT SHOULD
THE CHURCHES DO
ABOUT SOCIAL PROBLEMS?

HOWARD E. KERSHNER

President of the Christian Freedom Foundation, Howard Kershner was born in Kansas, graduated from Friends University and later studied economics at Harvard. After twenty-four years of varied business activities, he retired in 1938 to become Executive Vice-President of the International Commission for the Relief of Refugee Children in Europe. This work was supported by 24 governments. Later he organized and was President of the temporary council on Food for Europe's Children and was a member of the Executive Committee of Mr. Hoover's Committee on Food for the Small Democracies. He served as a member of the first board of directors of CARE.

As Vice-President of the Save the Children Federation, he set up the postwar program of that organization in Europe. This included some help to about six thousand destroyed schools extending from Finland to Italy and Greece. For one year, (1947-48) he served as Special Representative of the Secretary General of United Nations seeking grants for the Children's Emergency Fund. Several governments responded with grants running as high as $1 million.

Howard E. Kershner was one of the organizers of the Christian Freedom Foundation (1950). He founded and edits the fortnightly journal, *Christian Economics*. For twelve years he wrote the Sermonettes for this paper. They are used in the calendars or bulletins of more than 1500 churches throughout the nation, making a total circulation of about 450,000. His syndicated column, "It's Up To You," is now used in several hundred daily and weekly newspapers. He has written several books. Two of the most recent are *God, Gold and Government* and *Diamonds, Persimmons and Stars*. His weekly "Commentary on the News" is now aired by over 340 radio stations. His radio work, extending at times into Canada, South America and Europe, has also included television.

He was decorated with the Order of Leopold by the Belgian Government, the French Legion of Honor and the Palm d'Academie by the French Government. He has been cited six times by the Freedoms Foundation in Valley Forge, one of which was a first prize. He holds an honorary Doctorate of Humane Letters from Washington Jefferson College, an LL.D. from Friends University and Litt.D. from Grove City College.

He has carried his investigations into some threescore countries throughout the world. He writes for magazines and has acted as narrator in two documentary films, one of which was widely televised. For thirty years he has criss-crossed the nation as a speaker in churches, schools, colleges, seminaries and clubs. In religion he is a member of the Society of Friends and for five years was Clerk of New York Yearly Meeting. He has contributed many articles to Quaker journals.

WHAT SHOULD
THE CHURCHES DO
ABOUT SOCIAL PROBLEMS?

by Howard E. Kershner

Life was hard in my youth and early manhood. My hard-working, God-fearing parents lost all in droughts and grasshopper plagues of western Kansas during the closing decades of the past century. I have known hunger, cold, insufficient clothing and unheated housing without running water. There is little about poverty that I do not understand from personal experience. Later, my wife and I spent 10 years bringing some relief to starving and homeless people in Europe during the civil war in Spain, World War II, and in the postwar period when I was a member of the first Board of Directors of CARE, Vice President of Save the Children Federation, Director of the International Commission for Refugees and **special representative of Secretary General** Trygve Lie of the United Nations, seeking grants for the Children's Emergency Fund of that organization. I have witnessed starvation on a wholesale scale and vast numbers of people deprived of housing, medical care, and all the essentials of anything beyond a mere physical existence.

My sympathies are with suffering people and I have spent a good part of my life trying to help the unfortunate. Those who would have the church make pronouncements and take positions on social, political and economic questions cannot possibly be more interested in reaching these desirable goals than I. We need waste no time in discussing the need for relieving poverty and lifting the burden of misery from the backs of men. We agree on goals. We divide sharply on the best ways of making progress toward them.

When I say it is a great mistake for the minister, speaking from his pulpit, to take a position on one side or the other of sharply controversial economic, social and political problems, I am not saying that he should not discharge his duty as a citizen in these matters. He has the same secular means of doing so that are available to the rest of us. Church bodies should not make pronouncements in these areas and church papers should not publish editorials assuming that all people who are really Christians must take this or that view of current problems. To do so will divide the church for there is room for much difference of opinion regarding most social, economic and political problems. Equally honest and devoted Christian men and women will disagree about tariffs, monetary policy, agricultural problems, federal subsidies to schools, housing, relief, segregation, foreign aid, and many other problems. Equally consecrated Christians do not agree as to the will of God in these areas and if the church undertakes to speak *ex cathedra* concerning them it will divide its membership and lose its influence. Some Christian people are very certain they know what the role of the Federal Government should be regarding the recognition of Communist countries, but other equally concerned Christians are not so sure that their brethren know the will of God in foreign relations.

When the minister leads their thinking in the spiritual realm two men of opposing views may worship in harmony side by side in the pew,

but if he proclaims a specific position regarding any of the controversial questions just mentioned, and many others, he will alienate a large
portion of his flock and the two men sitting side
by side will feel enmity rather than harmony.
One may be pleased by the sermon, and the other
made extremely unhappy. One will feel that the
minister does not know what he is talking about.
He will believe that the minister lacks information and that he has based his reasoning on false
premises and therefore arrived at erroneous
conclusions. That this is happening widely
throughout our country is evidenced by the lack
of church attendance and by the fact that many
churches have withdrawn their support from
church councils and their own denominational
leadership. Many others have withheld contributions or cut down their contributions because
the church is spending money for purposes that
they believe to be wrong.

Jesus commanded us to go into all the world
and preach the gospel to every creature. He did
not command us to go into the world and organize
peace corps or civil disobedience demonstrations. He did not resort to law or coercion as a
means of improving society. Such things are all
right in their place, but they are secular and
mundane. The church should operate in the eternal spiritual world.

John the Baptist said of Jesus, "Behold, the
Lamb of God which taketh away the sin of the
world." He did not say to behold the great leader
of social reform who will bring about justice and
the equalization of wealth. He said nothing about
strikes, subsidies, controls, emergency peace
campaigns, vigils, sit-ins, or teach-ins. If he had
based His appeal on any of the popular ideologies
of the day, His memory would hardly have out-

lasted a generation, but because He moved in a
very high spiritual plane, His message has come
ringing down through the centuries for 2,000
years. Let the preacher, the church council and
the religious paper do likewise and the two men
with differing sociological, economic and political views may worship together in harmony and
join with each other and their church in the pro-
mulgation of the Christian Gospel, which is the
power of God unto salvation.

I am not saying that these social, economic
and political questions are not important or that
Christians should not concern themselves might-
ily with them. They are important and every
Christian should be concerned, but our concern
and our actions should be taken through secular
organizations and not through the churches.

We need to get our hearts right through the
worship of God and then mobilize our secular
organizations to take the required action for the
improvement of society. The church is not the
proper instrumentality to that end and if we attempt to use it for that purpose we shall destroy
it. We have political parties, chambers of commerce, labor unions, parent-teacher associa-
tions, service clubs, and many organizations
through which we can work for the improvement
of society. We need not desecrate and degrade
the church for that purpose.

When spiritual rebirth takes place, through
repentance, and forgiveness of one's sins, growth
in Grace is continued through persistent worship
of God, and the high ethical standards which we attribute to Him become the ruling principles of
our lives. Reborn men and women go out and
remake society. I am just as much interested in
meeting social needs and solving economic problems as my Socialist friends, but I insist that

we must not try to do it by changing our churches into social action agencies. They must not climb down from the spiritual plane. They must not take sides on controversial questions of economics and politics. Such matters are temporal. They shift from time to time. The church is a divine, permanent agency dealing with eternal principles and not with the temporary application thereof in the material world.

When the rich young ruler turned away sorrowful because he was not ready to surrender his life and his possessions to the will of Christ, Jesus might have said to His disciples that the young man does not know that is good for him, so draw up a law that will dispossess him of the greater part of his wealth and we will use it properly. If Jesus had taken that attitude we would never have heard of Him. If the church descends to the basis of dividing wealth and promoting socialism, it will become as short-lived as our secular organizations. To remain permanent, it must be a divine institution proclaiming eternal spiritual principles.

When one of a company of people who were listening to Jesus said to Him, "Master, speak to my brother, that he divide the inheritance with me," Jesus replied, "Man, who made me a judge or a divider over you?" Then Jesus said to the people, "Take heed, and beware of covetousness . . ." (Luke 12:13-15).

That saying has a meaning for the church today. It does not mean that we should not be good trustees to God both with our time and our means. It is the duty of our ministers and our church leaders to seek to inculcate in all of us a sense of trusteeship. On the other hand, if Jesus himself refused to be "a judge or a divider over you," it would seem altogether out of place for the church to assume those roles.

The proponents of the so-called Social Gospel say, "How can a Christian ignore the great need?" He can't. He will be greatly concerned and he will do his utmost to bring about improvement, but he will do this by secular means and not by seeking to make a wrongful use of a sacred divine institution established by Jesus Christ for the purpose of operating permanently in the spiritual world.

Our so-called liberal friends often speak contemptuously of pious people. They say that individual piety counts for little, and has no bearing on the great sociological issues of integration, housing, education and equalization of wealth. They are wrong. If the church had fulfilled its mission, taught the people to worship God and respect His moral law summarized in the Ten Commandments, our present seemingly insoluble problems would not exist. The only way to cure poverty is to improve the character of individuals.

Slums and People

We can't get people out of the slums until we get the slums out of the people. Take the people out of the slums and they will create more slums wherever they are just as we have more delinquency and crime in some of our low-cost housing developments in New York City than in other parts of the city. Moving people with unregenerated hearts into a good, new clean apartment doesn't change character and they will soon make a slum of it.

To conquer poverty we must regenerate people one by one; that is, promulgate the personal piety which the welfare staters ridicule. For example, the people waste more money in foolish,

harmful practices than ever can be spent by government for improving their condition. Some $20
billion a year is wasted for tobacco and liquor
in our country and at least an equal sum for
gambling, not to mention other wasteful frivol-
ities. We cannot possibly spend $40 billion a
year of public funds to cure poverty, but a substantial portion of that sum could be saved by the
poor people themselves if they became wor-
shippers of God, reverently keeping his Commandments.

Let no one say that I wish to coerce or control
people in the expenditure of their incomes. It is
not my purpose to say to anyone that he should
not smoke, drink or gamble. If an adult can pay
for such things himself, that is his business, but
he has no right to make me pay for these or the
crime and poverty flowing from them, or to
raise and educate his children for him because
he has wasted his own resources. The point is
that if the power of the Gospel enters the human
heart, most people will become self-reliant and
self-supporting. They will be thrifty, honest,
truthful and will refrain from coveting and stealing. That is the only way to solve the social
problems which confront us. If the church deserts
her moral and spiritual leadership and descends
to the material plane, there is little hope of improving the wretched conditions that exist
throughout so large a portion of the world.

A Shocking Statement

I recently heard a liberal Christian leader
speak of the "dedicated, high-principled young
men who surrounded Castro in his move for
social justice in Cuba." This shocking statement
shows what happens when religious leaders begin
to place their faith in material movements and

reforms. That a minister of the Gospel should find comfort or take satisfaction in crass, Godless, materialistic communism is extremely disquieting. So was his statement that the personal habits of individuals such as smoking, drinking, gambling and sleeping with another man's wife were trivial when compared with the great social issues of integration and equalization of wealth. I do not regard sleeping with another man's wife as trivial. The fact is that a decline of sexual integrity has always accompanied the disintegration of civilization. Society cannot be cleansed by social reform or by the movement of history. This can be done only by spiritual rebirth and the cleansing of the human heart through faith in, and obedience to, the will of God. Our difficulties have arisen because the church has deserted its true mission. A nation of pious people is not troubled by an oversupply of criminals, sex perverts, dope addicts, drunks, delinquents and broken homes.

When John Calvin went to Geneva it was one of the most depraved cities in Europe. He constantly reminded his ministers to concentrate on proclaiming the spiritual message of the church. This was done and within the space of a few years Geneva became one of the most wholesome and best-governed cities in Europe. Today the church has taken the opposite direction and has brought tragedy and disaster upon us.

Faith in God that remakes character is the answer to most of our social problems. As Isaiah (50:7) expresses it: "For the Lord God will help me; therefore shall I not be confounded: therefore have I set my face like a flint, and I know that I shall not be ashamed."

Nothing but faith in God can cause a man to set his face like a flint, to overcome his temptation and to be truthful, honest and just in all his dealings. This transformation takes place in the spiritual world, and is the function of the church. It cannot be done in the material world and when the church descends to that plane, the best hope of fundamental improvement in society disappears. When the church places its faith in coercive governmental action, it is bound to be defeated. Government can control people and drive them like slaves, but it cannot regenerate their hearts. Without the latter, there is no internal, redeeming self-help through the renewal of a right spirit within man. Until this change takes place, the best we can hope for is a coercive society, with a strongly centralized government and discipline through the action of the secret police. In the end, it means a master and slave relationship.

Faith in God puts courage and determination into the hearts of men. These are the qualities that conquer poverty and solve other social problems. It is the business of the church to mobilize spiritual power. By doing so, it can solve our perplexing social and economic problems, but if if deserts its true function and places its trust in the puny forces which men may assemble through their own institutions, it will meet with continuing tragic failure. When the state does things for people, they lose the power to help themselves, but when through faith in God they make a mighty effort to solve their own problems, most of them are successful. This principle is well illustrated by the story of the sea gulls who lived from the waste of the fish cannery. In time, they grew fat and lazy and were unable to find food for themselves. When the cannery closed, they starved to death. The greatest evil that can be perpetrated against the

American people is to teach them to depend upon
the state until they lose initiative, self-reliance
and character. That is the way to permanent
enslavement.

The church must choose to depend upon and
to invoke divine power which knows no limit
and overcomes every obstacle or to place its
faith in the feeble efforts of man. Let us hope
that it will recover from its temporary obses-
sion with man-made institutions, and quickly
rise again to the spiritual level, resuming its
proper function of proclaiming the Gospel of
Christ as the means of individual salvation — the
only road to the solution of our social problems.

When the church takes a position on secular
questions it becomes involved in untenable and
ridiculous situations. For instance, some years
ago, when I was having a discussion with the
Minister of Finance in Lebanon, he told me that
his country had no inflation, no indebtedness,
always balanced its budget and had a sound monetary unit which was not losing its purchasing
power. After congratulating him, I said, "Will
you tell me, Mr. Minister, why my country which
has balanced its budget only 6 times in the past
33 years, suffers from chronic inflation, owes
more money than all the rest of the governments
of the world put together and suffers from a de-
preciating dollar — will you tell me, Mr. Minister, why we should continue to give your
country tens of millions of dollars a year?" He
replied, "I know of no reason why you should do
so, but if you wish to do it, of course we will be
glad to have it." To the man who knows that much
of the $130 billion our country has paid out in
foreign aid since World War II has been worse
than wasted and that some of it finds its way into
numbered accounts in Lebanon and Switzerland —

to hear his church continually advocating more of
the same is too much, and many church members
have been lost on that issue.

In like manner, the church is backing the
Appalachian program for the relief of poverty
in that area. I was in Spartanburg, South Carolina, recently and was told that the unemployment
rate in that county was only about half of the
average for the nation and that the county was
experiencing a real boom. Nevertheless, the
Federal Government insists that the people in
Spartanburg County, South Carolina, are poor
and that it must submit to being a part of the
Appalachian program. Good church people of that
area are up in arms. For the church to champion
these questionable controversial measures which
may appear right one day and wrong the next is
to become involved in statements and positions
that appear ridiculous and bring great disfavor
upon it.

A large part of the church leadership in the
United States has urged the recognition of Communist China and the admission of that country
to the United Nations. Probably an overwhelming
portion of church membership is opposed to that
course and has been made very unhappy by the
action of their spokesmen.

A large portion of our church leaders approved
of the stalemate in Korea and of the rejection of
General MacArthur's plea for permission to
inflict a complete rout upon the Communist
enemy. This also brought great disfavor upon the
church.

To the regret and disgust of perhaps the major
portion of the church membership our country,
much of our church hierarchy backed the Castro
movement for the communization of Cuba. When
secular organizations advocate such measures

and are proven to be wrong, no great damage is done for they are of a temporary nature and may be supplanted by others that are able more accurately to interpret the will of the people. But when our one permanent divine institution deserts its commission to preach the Gospel and makes such grievous blunders in secular affairs, it suffers irreparable damage. Moreover, in so doing it often violates the moral law of God which it is supposed to champion.

Divided Into Pressure Groups

Not long ago, I made a talk along these lines at a church dinner. In the question period, the minister of the church arose and explained that the railroads were increasing the monthly fare of his parishioners who work in New York to the extent of some $25. He said they could not afford to pay it, and that the government should do something about it. "What do you think the government should do?" I asked. After a moment's reflection he replied, "I think the government should subsidize the railroads." "That will mean," I answered, "that the government will go into the slums of New York and take money from people who have never been on a train, people who are obliged to live in the noisy, crowded, dirty city because they cannot afford to live in the suburbs and give this money to your parishioners so they can live in this far more pleasant community. If you are really honest you will advise your parishioners to take a piece of paper and write at the top: I cannot afford to pay my railroad fare. Will you contribute 50¢ or $1 a month so that I may continue to live in the suburbs while working in New York? "No one would sign a paper of that kind," the minister said. "Of course not," I replied, "But you propose to put your hand in the people's pockets and take the money from them and that is both coveting and stealing.

"Your parishioners will no more than have returned from their unsuccessful effort to obtain help for their railroad tickets than a group of farmers will knock on the door and, after you have invited them in, will explain that they cannot afford to sell their farm produce at the market price and will ask you to contribute a dollar a month so they may have more than the market affords. You will be sympathetic and will explain that you would like to help them, but that you have to pay your own grocery bill which is quite all you can manage. But you do help them for they organize a pressure group, go into politics and take $6 to $8 billion out of your pockets every year.

"After the farmers leave, another group will knock on your door and tell you that they want to build houses and ask you to help them financially? You will explain that you are having some difficulty paying for your own home and are unable to help them, but you do, for they go into politics and through pressure upon government succeed in getting subsidies in one way and another for most of our housing developments.

"Another group comes and asks for help in the payment of their rent. You say you have difficulties of your own but they likewise organize a pressure group and succeed in getting government to subsidize a large portion of the rental housing of our country.

"The oyster fishermen got into difficulty and petitioned government to subsidize oysters. Some years ago the scrap iron dealers were not getting enough for their scrap and petitioned government to stockpile scrap iron. At one time the egg

producers of South Jersey petitioned government
to start buying shell eggs. The government refused but the farmers said, 'You buy dried eggs,
milk, cream, butter, wheat, corn and many other
products. What have you got against shell eggs?''

The tragedy is that these measures, instituted
for temporary relief, often become a useful
political device that entraps both the original
benefactors and beneficiaries.

The farm program is a classical example. It
was started in 1933 to give temporary help to
farmers. It has solved no problem. Today the
same arguments used then are still being used to
keep such subsidy programs on the books. And
farmers on several occasions have voted over-
whelmingly against them. Last year Congressmen from wheat states voted 2 to 1 against the
wheat program. Yet big-government planners and
big city Congressmen forced it through.

The biggest voluntary farm organization in the
world has worked for 18 years to get government
out of the farmers' business, but the forces of
socialism are such that it has not yet been
successful.

The segment of agriculture that does not get
these massive subsidies is far healthier than the
others.

And so, we have divided ourselves into a vast
number of pressure groups, each coveting the
wealth of others and striving to see how much it
can obtain for itself. We have become a nation of
championship of the so-called welfare state, con-
ceived as a program for social justice, is violat-
ing and tearing down the very moral laws of God
which it is its duty to teach and proclaim to
people. A church which continues to do that cannot prosper and cannot for long retain the confidence, respect and love of the people. It has

failed in its mission of proclaiming the Gospel and is devoting its time to the impossible task of trying to divide up the wealth and redistribute it among the people. It does not seem to understand that when the time and attention of the people is centered upon dividing wealth — that is, getting some of the wealth of others — that they are not concentrating on the production of wealth. Consequently, the assembly lines slow down and less wealth is created.

The socialism, which much of our church leadership is advocating for our country, and the appeasement and wasteful foreign aid program it urges for friend and foe alike are recognized by a large part of our church membership as threatening the very solvency and even the life of our country. If our church leadership continues to pontificate in this realm it will greatly injure the church. Even though it might give the right advice, it would still divide the church for there are many who will not agree.

To stay united, the church should remain on the spiritual plane seeking to cancel out sin and leave to reborn men and women the secular problems of meeting human need and improving society. In that manner, the church can recover its mighty influence over men and women, can point the way to salvation from sin and so achieve a happy, prosperous and self-governing free society. The alternative is to lead us deeper into socialism with its accumulating miseries.

Appendix

Reference Notes to the Text

INTRODUCTION

1. See *Methodist Laymen*, North Hollywood, January 22, 1964.
2. *This Week* magazine, July 18, 1965.
3. *Monthly Messenger*, McKeesport, Pa., June, 1965.
4. *Gainesville* (Florida) *Independent*, August 4, 1965.

CHAPTER I

1. Chambers, Whittaker, *Witness*, Random House, New York, 1952, p. 17.
2. "The American Clergy and the Basic Truths," *Christianity Today*, Washington, D. C., Vol. v, Number 1, October 10, 1960, p. 27.
3. Mackay, John A., *Presbyterian Life*, July 15, 1961.
4. Ely, Richard T., *Ground Under Our Feet*, Macmillian, New York, 1938, p. 111.
5. Sullivan, Lawrence, "Socialism by Stealth," *Christian Economics*, September 21, 1965, p. 1.
6. Ely, *The Social Law of Service*, Eaton and Mains, New York, 1896, p. 20.
7. Ely, *The Social Aspects of Christianity*,

Thomas Y. Crowell and Co., New York, 1889, p. 60.

8. Ely, *The Social Law of Service*, p. 167.

9. *Ibid.*, p. 165.

10. *Ibid.*, ch. 9.

11. Dorfman, Joseph, *The Economic Mind in American Civilization*, The Viking Press, New York, 1959, Vol. iii, p. 162.

12. Gladden, Washington, *Recollections*, Houghton Mifflin Co., Boston, 1909, p. 265.

13. Atkins, Gauis Glenn and Fagley, Frederick L., *History of American Congregationalism*, Pilgrim Press, Boston, 1942, pp. 251-252.

14. Gladden, *Applied Christianity*, Houghton Mifflin Co., Boston, pp. 69-70.

15. Gladden, *Social Facts and Forces*, New York and London, 1897, p. 203.

16. Baker, Ray Stannard, *The Social Unrest*, New York, 1910 p. 268.

17. Bodein, Vernon P., *The Social Gospel of Walter Rauschenbusch*, Yale University Press, New Haven, 1944, pp. 3-4.

18. Rauschenbusch, Walter, *Christianizing the Social Order*, Macmillan, New York, 1912, p. 439.

19. Edman, Dr. V. Raymond, *Bulletin of Wheaton College*, October 1952, Vol. 29, No. 7.

20. Rauschenbusch, *Theology for the Social Gospel*, Macmillan, New York, 1917, p. 184.

21. *Ibid.*, p. 179-180.

22. Visser 't Hooft, *The Background of the Social Gospel*, Oxford University Press, 1928, p. 178.

23. *Zion's Herald*, July 4, 1923, pp. 849-850.

24. *Hearings*, House Committee on Un-American Activities, July 7, 8, 13 and 14, 1953, pp. 2084-2085.

25. *Hearings,* House Committee on Un-American Activities, July 7, 8, 13 and 14, 1953 p. 2266.
26. *Ibid.,* p. 2142.
27. Burton, Malcolm, *Destiny for Congregationalism,* Modern Publishers, Inc., Oklahoma City, 1953, p. 131.
28. Miller, Robert Moats, *American Protestantism and Social Issues,* University of North Carolina Press, Chapel Hill, 1958, p. 78.
29. *World Tomorrow,* May 10, 1934, p. 219.
30. Miller, *op.cit.,* p. 97.
31. Kegley, Charles W. and Bretall, Robert W., Ed., *Reinhold Niebuhr — His Religious, Social, and Political Thought,* Macmillan, New York, 1956, p. 435.
32. *Hearings,* House Committee on Un-American Activities, July 21, 1953, passim.
33. *The Worker,* May 23, 1965.
34. Heilbroner, Robert L., *The Worldly Philosophers,* Simon and Schuster, New York, 1953, p. 259.
35. Roepke, Wilhelm, *The Moral Foundation and Impact of Keynesianism,* Education Division, National Association of Manufacturers, New York, 1965, p. 8.

CHAPTER 2

1. Leonard Gross, "America's Mood Today," *Look,* June 29, 1965, 18.
2. *San Francisco Examiner,* January 18, 1965.
3. *U. S. News and World Report,* May 23, 1962, 90.
4. *Ibid.,* September 13, 1965.
5. *Ibid.,* August 2, 1965.
6. *Ibid.,* August 9, 1965.

7. Billy Graham, *World Aflame* (Garden City, New York: Doubleday & Company, Inc., 1965), 3.

8. David L. McKenna, "The Moral Revolution and The Christian College," *Christianity Today*, July 19, 1964, 10.

9. Quoted in "Will Sex Destroy America?" *Christian Economics*, April 30, 1957. See also Pitrim A. Sorokin, "The Depth of the Crisis: American Sex Morality Today," *Christianity Today*, July 4, 1960, 3-5. Here Sorokin answers Crane Brinton who writes in his *A History of Western Morals*, 386, that modern American sex morality is "rather stricter than at many periods in Western history." Sorokin presents over-whelming evidence of a greater looseness of sex morality.

10. Howard E. Kershner, *Christian Economics*, December 10, 1963.

11. *U. S. News and World Report*, May 31, 1965.

12. Jeffrey St. John, "SMUT Two Billion Dollar A Year Racket," *Our Sunday Visitor*, September 5, 1965, 4.

13. Circulation Of Obscene And Pornographic Material. Hearing Before the Subcommittee On Postal Operations, May 27, 1960, 3.

14. Daniel Lyons, "Man-Made Morals," *Our Sunday Visitor*, August 22, 1965.

15. Brock Chisholm, *Prescription For Survival*, Bampton Lectures in America Delivered at Columbia University 1957, (New York: Columbia University Press, 1957, Third Printing, 1964), 55.

16. Quoted in Arthur H. DeKruyter, "Do Humanists Exploit Our Tensions?" *Christianity Today*, April 28, 1958, 3.

17. *The National Observer*, July 19, 1965, 15.

269

18. *Ibid.*
19. *Ibid.*
20. Stacey Hebdon Taylor, "The New Legality," *The Canadian Intelligence Service,* August, 1965, Supplementary Section, 2.
21. *The Torch,* October 20, 1964.
22. William Graham Cole, *Called To Responsible Freedom: The Meaning of Sex in the Christian Life,* copyright by the National Council of Churches, 1961, 5, 9, 10, 11, 13.
23. Robert C. Buckle, "Love Without Fear — A Personal View of Being Physical," Vol. 3, No. 4. *United Campus Christian Fellowship Publication,* 1720 Chouteau Avenue, St. Louis 3, Missouri.
24. *Ibid.*
25. John A. T. Robinson, *Honest To God* (Philadelphia: The Westminster Press, 1963), 118. *Honest To God* has received considerable favorable publicity in the religious press. The book was favorably reviewed in the August 26, 1964 *Lutheran* and the Autumn, 1963, *Dialog,* 271. *National Review,* June 2, 1964, 453, said in its review titled "Death of God in Modern Theology:" "*Honest To God* represents a serious Protestant attempt to realize Nietzsche's assertion, 'God is dead. You have killed Him'"
26. *Ibid.,* 119.
27. *Ibid.,* footnote #1. Soundings is a symposium edited by A. R. Vidler and published by the Cambridge University Press, 1962. Vidler is dean of King's College, England.
28. Howard Carson Blake, " 'The New Morality,' " *Christianity Today,* March 27, 1964, 8.
29. *Time,* March 5, 1965.
30. *The Christian Century,* March 31, 1965.

31. *Ibid.* For the testimony of Herbert Philbrick on Reverend Joseph Fletcher of the Episcopal Theological Seminary see the House Committee on Un-American Activities report "Investigation Of Communist Activities In The New York City Area — Part 5," July, 1953, pp. 2017-2018. Philbrick testified: "Joe Fletcher worked with us on Communist Party projects and on enormous number of tasks."

32. *Christian Economics*, November 17, 1964.

33. *Christianity And Crisis*, January 25, 1965.

34. *Christianity Today*, April 23, 1965.

35. *The Sword Of The Lord*, November 6, 1964.

36. *The Honest To God Debate* (Philadelphia: The Westminster Press, 1963), 181. The article in this volume by Theodore O. Wedel was reprinted from *The Episcopalian*.

37. *U. S. News and World Report*, July 20, 1964.

38. *St. Louis Globe Democrat*, October 23, 1964.

39. Martin Luther King is more of a humanist than a Christian theologian. He does not affirm with dogmatic certainty basic Christian doctrines. See Religion in Action, a Newsbook by *The National Observer*, 1965, 128, 129.

40. Operation Understanding edition of *Our Sunday Visitor*, March 28, 1965, 1.

41. "Senator Raps Clergymen For Aiding Violence," *St. Louis Globe Democrat*, August 25, 1965.

42. *U. S. News and World Report*, July 5, 1965, 60.

43. John 14:15.

44. John 14:24.

45. Matthew 5:17-19.

46. 1 Corinthians 6:13, 15, 18. See also Galatians

5:19-21; 1 Corinthians 3:5-8; 1 Thessalonians 4:3-7; 1 Corinthians 5:9-13.
47. Romans 1:22-32.
48. Romans 13:1. See also 1 Peter 2:13-17.

CHAPTER X

1. Hadvan Koht: *Driving Forces in History*, p. 194. Einar Haugen, translator. Cambridge, Massachusetts: Belknap Press of Harvard University Press, 1964.
2. Erich Kahler: *Man the Measure, A New Approach to History*, p. 639f. New York: Braziller, 1961.
3. M. D. Conway: *The Rejected Stone: or, Insurrection vs. Resurrection in America*, pp. 76, 113, 115. Boston: Walker, Wise, 1862, third edition.
4. O. B. Frothingham: *The Religion of Humanity*, p. 20. New York: G. P. Putnam's Sons, 1875; third edition. See R. J. Rushdoony: *The Nature of the American System*, chapter VI, "The Religion of Humanity," a study of this movement; Nutley, New Jersey: The Craig Press, 1965.
5. Charles Ferguson: *The Religion of Democracy, A Memorandum of Modern Principles*, p. 93. New York and London: Fund & Wagnalls, 1900.
6. *The Arena*, vol. XXV, no. 4, April, 1901. p. 458.
7. Charles Ferguson: *The University Militant*, p. 8. New York and London: Mitchell Kennerley, 1911.
8. Charles Ferguson: *The Great News*, preface. New York: Mitchel Kennerley, 1915.
9. Ferguson: *The Religion of Democracy*, pp. iii, 7ff., 17, cf. 46.

272

10. *Ibid.*, p. 33.
11. *Ibid.*, p. 80.
12. *Ibid.*, p. 35.
13. *Ibid.*, p. 55.
14. *Ibid.*, p. 98.
15. *Ibid.*, p. 169.
16. *Ibid.*, p. 37.
17. *Ibid.*, p. 40.
19. *Ibid.*, p. 58.
20. *Ibid.*, pp. 91ff., 97.
21. *Ibid.*, p. 149.
22. *Ibid.*, p. 152f.
23. *Ibid.*, p. 153ff.
24. *Ibid.*, p. 155.
25. Charles Ferguson: *The Affirmative Intellect, An Account of the Origin and Mission of the American Spirit*, p. 8. New York and London: Funk and Wagnalls, 1901.
26. *Ibid.*, p. 40.
27. *Ibid.*, p. 59.
28. *Ibid.*, p. 125.
29. *Ibid.*, p. 152.
30. *Ibid.*, p. 127.
31. Ferguson: *The University Militant*, p. 20f.
32. *Ibid.*, p. 67.
33. *Ibid.*, p. 76.
34. *Ibid.*, p. 124.
35. Charles Ferguson: *The Great News*, p. 41.
36. *Ibid.*, p. 204.
37. Charles Ferguson: *The Revolution Absolute*, p. 27f. New York: Dodd, Mead, 1918.
38. Charles S. Macfarland: *Christian Unity in Practice and Prophecy*, p. 53. New York: Macmillan, 1933.
39. *Ibid.*, p. 56f.
40. William O. Douglas: *Freedom of the Mind*,

p. 36. *Readings for An Age of Change,* no. 3. Published by the American Library Association in cooperation with the Public Affairs Committee, New York, 1962.

41. Cornelius Van Til: *The New Modernism, An Appraisal of Theology of Barth and Brunner,* p. 275. Philadelphia: The Presbyterian and Reformed Publishing Company, 1946.

42. Thomas J. J. Altizer: *Mircea Eliade and the Dialectic of the Sacred,* p. 13. Philadelphia: The Westminster Press, 1963. Other leaders in this movement include Prof. Paul Van Buren of Temple, Gabriel Vahanian of Syracuse, the Jewish scholar Dr. Richard L. Rubenstein, Dr. William Hamilton of Colgate-Rochester Divinity School, and others. See William Hamilton, "The Death of God Theology", in *The Christian Scholar,* vol. XLVII, no. 1, Spring, 1965, pp. 27-48; Richard L. Rubenstein, "Person and Myth in the Judaeo-Christian Encounter", *The Christian Scholar,* XLVI, no. 4, Winter, 1963, pp. 278-292; Gabriel Vahanian: The Death of God, The Culture of our Post-Christian Era, New York: Braziller, 1961; Terry Southern, Richard Seaver, Alexander Trocchi, editors: *Writers in Revolt, An Anthology,* pp. 11-17, "Introduction: Toward the Ethics of a Golden Age", New York: Berkeley Medallion Books, 1965.

43. T. George Harris, "The Battle of the Bible", in *Look,* July 27, 1965, Vol. 29, no. 15, pp. 17-20.

44. *Ibid.,* p. 19.

45. "Example of the Cloth", reprinted in *U. S. News and World Report,* August 2, 1965, Vol. LIX, no. 5, p. 84.

46. Quoted and reviewed in the editorial, "The New Confession: A Responsible Critique", in *Christianity Today*, Vol. IX, no. 22, July 30, 1965, 1. 32. (1124).

47. Louis Baldwin, "The Irrelevance of Vatican II", in *The Catholic World*, Vol. 201. no. 1, 204, July, 1965, p. 261n.

48. Mother Maria Carl Haipt, O. S. U.: *The Social Aspects of the Christian Faith Contained in Mater et Magister and Pacem in Terris*, p. 79, Glen Rock, New Jersey: Paulist Press Deus Books, 1964.

49. Robert W. Gleason, S. J.: *The Immorality of Segregation*, p. 16f., Paulist Press: 1961, reprinted from Joseph E. O'Neill, S. J., editor, *A Catholic Case Against Segregation*, Macmillan, 190.

50. Avery Dulles, S. J.: Ecumenism: *A Catholic Concern*, p. 24. New York: Paulist Press, 1962.

51. Sergio Mendez Arcea, "The Church, an Open Community", in Hans Kung, Yves Congar, O. P., and Daniel O'Hanlon, S. J., editors: *Council Speeches of Vatican II*, p. 182f. Glen Rock, New Jersey: Paulist Press, 1964.

52. *Ibid.*, p. 183.

53. Augustin Cardinal Bea: *Unity in Freedom, Reflections on the Human Family*, 211, Vol. 11 of Religious Perspectives. Ruth Nanda Anshen, editor, New York: Harper and Row, 1964.

54. *Ibid.*, p. 214f.

55. "Sabrepen": Proceeding from Pugwash to the "World of Disarmament", p. 2. McLean, Virginia: Sabrepen Syndicate, 1964.

56. *Christian Century*, July 11. 1945, p. 818, "Federal Council Approves Charter."

57. Stephen F. Bayne, Jr., Bishop of Olympia:
*The Faith, The Church and the University,
A Report of a Conversation Among University Christians*, p. 36. Cincinnati: Forward Movement Publications, 1959.